An Illustrated History of
LEICESTER'S RAILWAYS

By
John Stretton

IRWELL PRESS

Copyright Irwell Press
ISBN 1-871608-49-X

Contents

Front cover top. **On a dull, damp December day, the bay platforms at the south end of Leicester Central station are home to a strange locomotive pairing. There is earnest discussion on 15 December 1955 between loco crew (presumably off the B1) and a bowler-hatted official and no doubt there is some emergency needing solution. Wearing 'The South Yorkshireman' headboard, Leicester Central shed's B1 61188 is no doubt primed to take over this prestigious train, but there is no sign of the coaching stock. Precisely what part in the story is played by neighbour A3 60062** *Isinglass,* **is not known, but to see such a locomotive in the station bearing a King's Cross (34A) shedplate is indeed a rarity, although possibly it is on loan to another shed. 'The South Yorkshireman' ceased to operate from 2 January 1960.** *(P H Wells)*

Front cover lower. **At London Road station, there is no such mystery. On Saturday,29 August 1964, 'Jubilee' 45557,** *New Brunswick,* **but now unnamed and with only a month of life left, simmers gently in the early morning sunshine, waiting to take holidaymakers to sand, sea and bright lights, as the 8.25 a.m. excursion to Blackpool. In the background, a DMU stands by the recently-installed Fox Street fuel tank and servicing point, whilst on the next track 4F 44421 clings on to life as pilot. The engine was withdrawn just four months later, from Stoke (5D) shed, and the whole of the sidings complex was swept away in the 1980s, to make room for the mark of 'progress' - a car park. Fuel oil came in by rail from Immingham, except when the tank was running low and replenishment was late, at which time the 15C shedmaster perforce had to order a road tanker from a local merchant!** *(Horace Gamble)*

Rear cover. **A delightful view of the much-missed and oft-mourned (by local historians as well as railway enthusiasts and aficionados) Belgrave Road station. The opulence of the facilities, both passenger and freight, were grossly in excess of either actual or potential traffic throughout the life of the branch, but were testament to the grand ideas of the Great Northern Railway as it forged its way into the town. On 11 April 1952, a proliferation of J6s holds sway. Left, 64249 simmers between duty calls, whilst next door, 64200 double-heads with 64257, waiting to pull away with an excursion to Skegness. In a little over a decade, all three locomotives and all passenger trains from this station had disappeared.** *(Alec Ford)*

**First Published in the United Kingdom by
IRWELL PRESS 1998
59A, High Street, Clophill, Bedfordshire MK45 4BE
Printed in Huddersfield by The Amadeus Press**

Foreword

Back to a time when, despite the increasing 'straws in the wind' appearances of diesels following the 1955 Modernisation Plan, steam could still be found in true revenue-earning service throughout the country. In and around Leicester, thankfully, dieselisation came late and local spotters could be forgiven for thinking "it won't happen here"! Local trains still ran; small country stations were still operative, often acting as admittedly uneconomic parcels offices; and photographers did not have to chase miles around the countryside to obtain their steam fix. In the bright morning sunshine of Saturday, 21 July 1962, our photographer is situated (legally with a trackside permit) between passenger and freight lines, just to the north of Knighton Tunnel, to capture Standard 4-6-0 75061 heading for its home base as the 7.05 a.m. stopper from Burton-on-Trent. Allocated to Leicester (15C) at the time, it was later whisked away to Liverpool, to Aintree (27B) shed, from where it was withdrawn in February 1967, only 18 months from the very end of steam on BR. *(Horace Gamble)*

In the past half-century or so, thousands upon thousands of photographs and millions of words have been published on the subject of railways. And still they come! Not only in book form, such as this offering, but in an ever-increasing number of periodicals. Today's railway enthusiast, whatever his bent, is so very lucky to have such a wealth of historical and current information ever readily available. John Stretton grew up in such an enlightened world, but it was not always thus.

Before the Second World War, when I started my interest in the subject, there was a severe dearth of good books and only one worthwhile periodical. Two major railway societies issued magazines for the connoisseur, but there were no ABC-type stock books. My first ten years, from the age of two or thereabouts, were of the passive sort, enjoying what I saw before me, but not knowing one locomotive from the next - except that some seemed more exotic because they carried, in the main, attractive names, such as 'Andromeda' or 'Bucephalus'. It was not until I went to secondary school, where I met like-minded individuals, that my railway education blasted into orbit. It became not so much a hobby, more a way of life; an interest shared by John Stretton launching himself, with the inevitable ABC, straight into the loco-spotting phase while travelling by train daily to and from grammar school.

This city of ours, although not in the same league as Crewe, Swindon or Doncaster, nevertheless should rank alongside the great names of the past, to whit the Stockton & Darlington, or the Liverpool & Manchester. George and Robert Stephenson are names synonymous with the Leicester & Swannington, but its chief promoter John Ellis, three times mayor of Leicester, does not get the recognition he deserves. Neither does Clement Stretton (yes, a distant relation), the Victorian engineer who was an authority and author on the design of steam locomotives (and another Lord Mayor). He was overshadowed by Thomas Cook, who, though not a native, settled here and founded the world-wide touring business, following his pioneering railway excursion from Leicester to Loughborough in 1841. Another 'local lad made good' was the photographer S W A Newton (who had a shop in King Street, where my earliest films were processed). About one hundred years ago, he voluntarily set himself the task of photographing the whole of the construction of the then new Great Central Railway, in reality an extension of the Manchester, Sheffield and Lincolnshire Railway, for which students of the Railway have been grateful ever since. His negatives are now the preserve of the Leicester Museum Service and evidence of some of his work is contained within these pages. Some sixty/seventy years later, I and one or two other like-minded individuals from the Leicester Railway Society, with some of the same missionary zeal, embarked on 'crusades' to record on film something of the disappearing scene around our city. Newton's dedication has been emulated, albeit to a far lesser degree, by a vast army of passionate amateur photographers since, some of whose work (or play even!) is displayed in the following pages.

Since the advent of photography in the middle of the 19th century, it has been an essential dimension in the recording of history and particularly so for the railway scene. How much more would our publications be enriched had it been possible to photograph George Stephenson driving the first train out of Leicester on 17 July 1832, or Thomas Cook's private excursion to Loughborough on 5 July 1841, or Queen Victoria boarding a train at Campbell Street station in December 1843!

John Stretton has been addicted to this facet of the hobby for many years, attracted initially by the lure of the steam engine and its shed scenes, recording the changing panorama in the local environment. Together with the other photographers featured in this volume, he shows that no amount of writing can portray as vividly as pictures just how drastic have been the developments changing the traditionally romantic railway into a clinically slick business, and how the permanent way can so easily and speedily lose its permanence.

Horace Gamble, Ratby, Leicester

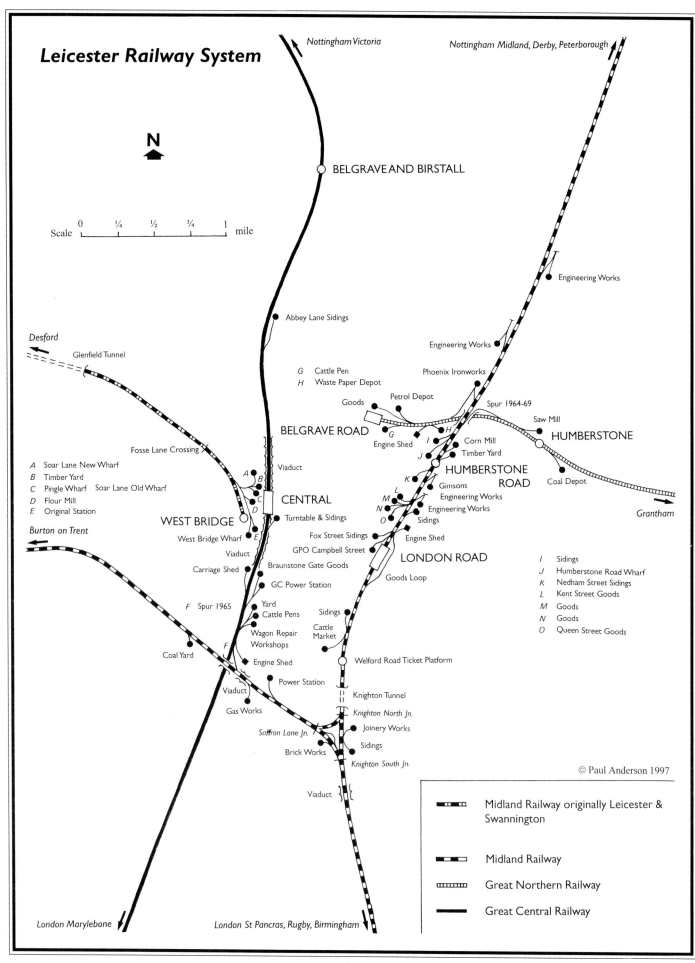

Leicester Railway System

N

Scale 0 ¼ ½ ¾ 1 mile

Nottingham Victoria

Nottingham Midland, Derby, Peterborough

BELGRAVE AND BIRSTALL

Engineering Works

Desford

Glenfield Tunnel

Abbey Lane Sidings

Engineering Works

G Cattle Pen
H Waste Paper Depot

Phoenix Ironworks

Goods Petrol Depot

Spur 1964-69 Saw Mill

Fosse Lane Crossing

BELGRAVE ROAD

Engine Shed G H I

HUMBERSTONE

A Soar Lane New Wharf
B Timber Yard
C Pingle Wharf Soar Lane Old Wharf
D Flour Mill
E Original Station

Viaduct

A
B
C

CENTRAL

Corn Mill
Timber Yard

J
HUMBERSTONE
ROAD

Coal Depot

Grantham

WEST BRIDGE

D

K
Gimsons
M Engineering Works

Burton on Trent

West Bridge Wharf

Turntable & Sidings

L

E
Viaduct

Fox Street Sidings

N Engineering Works
O Sidings

Carriage Shed

GPO Campbell Street

Engine Shed

LONDON ROAD

I Sidings
J Humberstone Road Wharf
K Nedham Street Sidings
L Kent Street Goods
M Goods
N Goods
O Queen Street Goods

Braunstone Gate Goods

GC Power Station

Goods Loop

F Spur 1965

Yard
Cattle Pens

Sidings

Wagon Repair
Workshops

Cattle
Market

Coal Yard

F

Engine Shed

Power Station

Welford Road Ticket Platform

Viaduct

Knighton Tunnel

Gas Works

Knighton North Jn.

Saffron Lane Jn.

Joinery Works

Sidings

Brick Works

Knighton South Jn.

© Paul Anderson 1997

Viaduct

London Marylebone

London St Pancras, Rugby, Birmingham

Midland Railway originally Leicester &
Swannington

Midland Railway

Great Northern Railway

Great Central Railway

Introduction

Like most people, I have an affinity with and affection for the place of my birth and although I am now separated from that place by both time and space, my loyalty is as strong as ever, (perhaps even more so, because of distance). I was born in Leicester and lived there for the first four years of my life, from 1943, before moving just four miles or so to the north, to Thurmaston. My interest in railways dates from 1955, a consequence of travelling to Loughborough to school by train and being influenced by many of my train-spotting colleagues. Whilst most of my spotting was done on the Midland main line at Thurmaston, I did venture, from the earliest times, to the Midland shed, courtesy of a friend of the family, and thence to the Central shed, cycling along the canal bank, annoying fishermen along the way, to attempt to bunk the rather gaunt looking edifice. Starting work in the city in 1961, I regularly visited 'the birdcage', overlooking the Midland shed, at lunchtimes, or tripped to the buffet on the Central station with friend Les, for a sandwich and Double Diamond. The railways of the area never let me down and the memories are countless, and still as vivid in many cases. The photographs I took in those days were less than perfect, but there were others more sophisticated than I, who took wonderful records of events and I have included some of them in this collection, to try and give a flavour of what the railways of Leicester meant to me, and indeed, to explain part of the love I have for the city, despite its many modern failings.

With origins that date back to pre-Roman times, Leicester for the past two hundred years has possessed an industrial rather than a fashionable reputation and even in the context of railway interest, local trainspotters would flock to the delights and excitements of Rugby, Nuneaton, Grantham or Derby, rather than stay in their own surroundings.

There has been much to witness since the first arrival of the railways in the town in the 1830s, from the Leicester & Swannington line, through the coming of the Midland and the Great Northern and then the entrance of the last main line, the Great Central. All have stories to tell, often mirroring, not surprisingly, the development of population growth and fluctuations in fortune of the many trades carried on within the town/city itself and the surrounding areas.

For my participation here in the examination of this procession of change, I have split the book into four parts, mirroring the distinct routes (and ex-railway companies) that were still in existence at the beginning of the 1960s. Each 'chapter' opens with a brief historical description. But this is merely an adjunct to the actual photographs and I shall feel satisfied if the reader merely enjoys their visual and pictorial impact.

During the preparation of this volume, I have had much and ready help from many individuals and my gratitude and sincere appreciation goes to all of them; but especial mention must be made of Horace Gamble, founder of the Leicester Railway Society half a decade or so ago, whose interest in the railways of Leicester, and his memory/knowledge of them and his involvement with them is both long-standing and truly impressive. Without his fund of photographs, his willingness to lend negatives for printing (several hundred were considered for this book!), and, perhaps above all, his readiness and ability to proof read my manuscript and pick me up on relevant and necessary points, the whole would have been so much the worse. I would also like to record my appreciation of Derek Mercer (darkroom wizard), Barry Hilton (another prolific photographer and trusting negative lender), Alec Swain (ex-Leicester shed master and caption proof reader), Irwell Press (for their tolerance with an author who did not always see things their way!), Paul Anderson (for his constant help, encouragement and map drawing abilities), but also, not least, my immediate family - who have demonstrated patience and encouragement during these past months of preparation.

JOHN STRETTON

Bibliography

**A Regional History of the Railways of Great Britain. Vol. 9
The East Midlands**. *Robin Leleux*. (David & Charles - 1976)

Forgotten Railways - The East Midlands. *P Howard Anderson*. (David & Charles - 1973)

Midland Main Line Memories. *Brian Radford*. (Midas Books - 1983)

The Midland Railway. *C Hamilton Ellis*. (Malaga Books - 1966)

Railways Around Leicester. *Horace A Gamble*. (Anderson Publications - 1989)

A Pictorial Record of the Leicester and Burton Branch Railway. *H N Twells*. (Trent Valley Publications - 1985)

History in Leicester. *Colin Ellis*. (City of Leicester Publicity Dept - 1969)

The Last Main Line. *R D Abbott*. (Leicester Museums - 1961)

John 'Railway' Ellis and his Family. *Margery Fishenden*. (Self-produced - 1992)

Leicestershire Railway Memories. *John Stretton*. (Unicorn Books - 1989)

30 Years of Trainspotting. *John Stretton*. (Unicorn Books - 1990)

Closely Observed Trains. *John Stretton*. (Silver Link Publishing - 1993)

Various articles from Railway Magazine and Railway World,
and various cuttings/news items collected over the years.

The Achilles Heel' of the Leicester-Swannington Railway - universally known latterly as 'the West Bridge branch' - was Glenfield Tunnel. The longest in the UK at the time, at 1796 yds., its height was severely restricted by geological factors and this meant that motive power was equally constrained throughout the lifetime of the branch. A number of carriages were specially built for the line, narrower than the norm and with bars on the *inside* of the drop windows, to prevent passengers decapitating themselves! In the very last years, BR Standard Class 2s took over the remaining traffic, with the two allocated to the duties having cut-down cabs. Less than a year before closure, suitably-doctored 78028, devoid of front number and shed plate, emerges from the eastern end of the Tunnel, with the Desford-West Bridge afternoon goods of Friday, 16 July 1965. *(Horace Gamble)*

CHAPTER ONE

WEST BRIDGE - GLENFIELD TUNNEL

Passengers never received premium service from the railway. From 1832 to 1887, intending travellers were accommodated in open trucks attached to goods trains (!) and no platform was provided at West Bridge until 1876. This latter was a very simple affair next to the Leicester Navigation and lasted until the provision of a more substantial structure on the far side of the goods yard, accessed from the then new King Richard's Road. This 'new' station , with its 'palatial' facilities of a waiting room, is seen on 3 May 1960, long after the demise of the passenger service, its platform road occupied by empty wagons awaiting their turn on the run westwards. *(Barry Hilton)*

Viewed from the vantage point of the dog days of the Millennium, and more than a century and a half from its origins, the Leicester & Swannington Railway is little thought of, if at all, by railway enthusiasts - let alone the great unwashed of the British public - and yet it had real significance; in at the dawn of the railway age and a tremendous influence for change in the fortunes of the county areas stretching out west from Leicester's town boundary. In Roman times, the whole line would have been without the city wall, this fortification being just over the water of the River Soar from what was to become the eastern terminus of the railway.

The birth pangs of the line have been well documented in various publications over the years, being inextricably linked with both of the Stephenson giants of the early railway movement and the Quaker Ellis family, by then domiciled in the pleasant Leicestershire countryside.

Originating at Dinnington, a village in Yorkshire, the Ellis Quaker 'dynasty' was large and widespread, including four generations of sons named James, with the one with which we are interested moving south to Leicestershire, from Beighton in Derbyshire, in 1758. He was ill at this stage and dependent on his son Joseph, who had moved south to rent Sharmans Lodge, on the Glenfield edge of Leicester Forest. Initially a farmer with £100 capital, he prospered, leasing more land and inhabiting a manor house and marrying into a Wigston Quaker family in 1788. One year later, his first son, John, was born - the first of six children -

growing up in the family house on land called Beaumont Leys, an area that is mentioned in the Domesday Book and which was bequeathed to Robert de Beaumont, when he was made the first Earl of Leicester by William the Conqueror.

In 1810, Joseph died, leaving the twenty-one year old John to take over the by now considerable and profitable estate. Although initially overawed by the responsibility, he followed the tenets of his father, progressing further the success of the estates and in turn becoming a magistrate, alderman, councillor and Liberal MP for Leicester, from 1848 to 1852. Being a successful businessman, it is perhaps not surprising that he was approached by a group of Leicester townsmen, prominent among them

Another view of the 'new' station, this time on 4 May 1963, with the buildings past the buffer stops, incorporating the booking office, facing down a longish approach road towards King Richard's Road. The platform and yard appear to be populated with non-railway merchandise. Probably the last visitation by a 'passenger' train to the platform, was the Leicester Railway Society's '25th Anniversary Special' of Saturday, 7 November 1964 - 78028 with a rake of half-a-dozen brakevans! *(R C Riley)*

colliery owner William Stenson of Whitwick, who were keen on improving the mode of shipment of coal from the rich seams of the Whitwick area to the homes and business of the town. Brought by horse and cart at that time, this was neither a swift, reliable or convenient method and thus, having given some initial thought to the possibilities of a canal and concerned lest their coal be upstaged by that from Nottinghamshire, these townsfolk turned to the idea of a railway, a form of transportation then being tried further north.

John's brother Joseph had already invested in George Stephenson's Liverpool & Manchester Railway and John was therefore recommended to approach this pioneer, to discuss the possibilities of a railway into Leicester. After some judicious marketing - he treated the great man to a good lunch! - and persuasive talking, aided by a map of the area, Stephenson was persuaded to visit the area, where he was impressed with the coalfield and the potential traffic. He declined to build a line himself, recommending rather that his son Robert undertake the task, but he was so impressed with the black gold and its potential, that he opened his own mine at Snibston, creating the village of Long Lane (later to become Coalville) and earning himself a small fortune!

At a meeting at the Bell Hotel in Leicester, on 12 February 1829, Robert accepted the undertaking, being appointed engineer and he soon began surveying, deciding, after consultation with his father, to retain the rail gauge already being used on the Stockton & Darlington, Liverpool & Manchester and Canterbury & Whitstable Railways. Finance for the line, (authorised capital of £90000 having to be subsequently raised to £140000),came from both the good townspeople of Leicester and business colleagues of George Stephenson in Liverpool and after the company had obtained its Act of Incorporation on 30 May 1830 - two and a half months ahead of the opening of the Liverpool & Manchester - construction progressed

Showing how little the traffic changed over the years, this view could have been the same day as top p.3, but is in fact three years earlier, on 27 April 1957. No doubt the good housewives of Tudor Road (right) are pleased to hang out their washing safe in the knowledge that there will not be many locomotives fouling the air around the station! In latter years, the platform waiting room had become a leather merchant's office. *(J F Clay)*

Moving slightly westwards from the platform, one of the staple diets of the branch traffic can be seen in the healthy supply of coal piled neatly to the left. This wider view of the terminus, seen in 1960, graphically shows the factories and terraced housing that graced this part of Leicester. The station buildings are dwarfed by, left, Bow Bridge Works (an elastic fabric manufacturer) and, right seen above the wagons, an Infants' School and King Richard III Secondary Girls School. The approach road to the booking office, etc. lay between the Works and the Schools. *(R S Carpenter)*

the longest in the country, at 1796 yds., it was also very limited in height, due to the nature of the earth above and the geographical problems encountered during construction, and this was to be a restricting feature of the working of the line right up until its closure well over a century later. Indeed, 'overseen' by Leicester Midland shed in its last years, the restrictions meant that the breakdown train was prohibited and in the event of a derailment, whatever re-railing equipment was required, jacks, wooden packing, etc., was loaded onto a specially ordered lorry which went to West Bridge by road! There had been plans to erect Mountsorrel granite portals at the tunnel mouths, from the local quarries, but due to the rising costs, these were abandoned. Locals still found it fascinating, however, and gates had to be installed at one period to keep them out!

The first engine for the line, 'Comet', built by Robert Stephenson & Co, in the Forth Works at Newcastle-upon-Tyne, was brought to West Bridge, the eastern terminus, on the banks of the River Soar, in kit form, first by boat to Hull and thence by canal, being assembled in a specially built shed. Initially an 0-4-0, it was later converted to 0-4-2, a trailing axle being added for stability. For the opening day, specially cleaned four-wheel wagons made up the train, with one 'roofed' for the day, for the Directors, who were all graced with chairs(!), and the other passengers being

without too much alarm, (although Daniel Jowett, one of the contractors did fall down one of the Tunnel's working shafts!), finally opening, with the inevitable Grand Opening celebrations, on 17 July, 1832. A line eastwards from West Bridge, across the River Soar, into the town was

authorised by Act of Parliament in 1833, but in reality this only ever saw realisation as a 22 chain branch to Soar Lane, opening in 1834. The only earthworks of note on the line, despite the undulating nature of the countryside, was the building of the Glenfield Tunnel. Then

Both type of locomotive and a particular example that saw long service on the branch. The Johnson 2F 0-6-0s were ideally suited to both branch and traffic, as they were able to (just) clear Glenfield Tunnel without adjustment, and with the freight work not requiring great speeds, often with limited loads, and there being no steep gradients on the way, they were able to take their time. They were also ideal for yard shunting, a duty being undertaken by 58143 (ex-MR 22955) on 5 May 1962 roughly in the middle of the yard complex, with Tudor Road to the right. Once provided by Leicester (Midland) shed, locomotives operating the line were latterly shedded at Coalville depot, from where 58143 was withdrawn in November 1963. *(R C Riley)*

The day before, picture bottom p.5, in equally dull conditions, 58143 is seen again on shunting duties. The lines to the left swung towards the Leicester Navigation, Soar Lane sidings and the original terminus platform. Note the water column, centre, fed by water from the purpose-built tower to its right. *(R C Riley)*

cossetted with planks in the coal wagons covered by green baize. A cannon was mounted in the rear wagon! On a bright 17 July 1832, the train, conveying some 400 souls, left the terminus, which had been advertised as Augustin Friars, at 10.00 a.m. for the near-eleven mile run to Bagworth, at that time the furthest completed point of the line. This first, 1832, station was at the foot on a 1-in-29 gravity-worked incline, which presented an early obstacle to the line and necessitated a 'deviation' - still at 1-in-66! - to be built some fifteen years later. George Stephenson himself came from Liverpool to drive this first train and the whole ensemble was treated to a champagne and cold 'collation' celebration

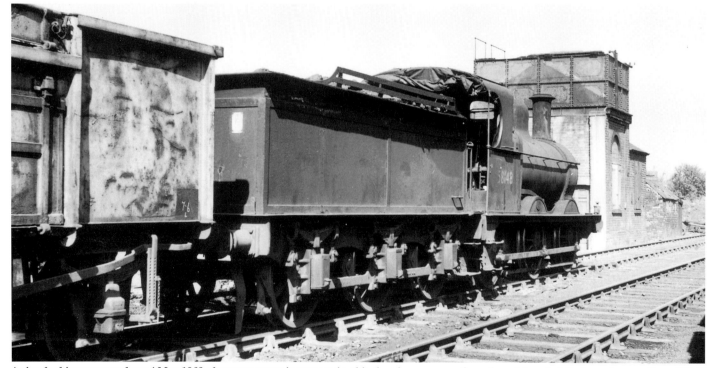

A view looking westwards on 4 May 1963, the water tower is seen again, this time in company of another stalwart of the branch operations, 58148 (ex-22967). The tower still bears the marks of the pitched roof of the old engine shed, built as a two-engine facility for the opening of the line but quickly extended. Like sister 58143, 58148 is one of the 1917-introduced Belpaire-firebox-fitted variant of Johnson's original 4' 11" design of 1875; again withdrawn from Coalville, the date this time was December 1963. Note the storm sheet fitted to the cab roof. Here not required and hence rolled up, the sheet could be lowered to protect the crew on reverse running, secured to the tender front by rope. Note also the once-ubiquitous steel-sided 16T wagon (giving greater carrying capacity than the 13T wooden versions used until the early 1960s) threatening to dwarf the loco. *(R C Riley)*

The same point as the last picture but one year later, on Saturday, 9 May 1964. The 2Fs having been withdrawn, ten-year-old Standard 2 2-6-0 78028 with cut-down cab has been drafted in to Coalville shed (denoted by the painted 15E plate on the smokebox). Shed codes were not cast in tablets of stone and changed to reflect alterations to Motive Power Districts and/or Regional boundaries. Once 17C, in the Derby District, the depot's code was 15D until the early 1960s, when it was interestingly 'swapped' with the 'Midlandised' Leicester Central shed, which then closed in July 1964. Hardly a cost-effective exercise! Coalville itself closed to steam on 4 October 1965. The driver of 78028 appears to be scratching his head as he rounds the tender of his charge; perhaps there was a problem with the loco, or the return CB6 (Coalville Branch 6) duty! *(Horace Gamble)*

in a marquee at Bagworth. The train had left to the sound of the cannon and this had been fired at each station along the route! - perhaps this was partly to reinforce the notice that had appeared in the local press the week before the trip, to the effect that, "It will be absolutely necessary that the Line of Railway should be kept clear, and the public are warned

that any persons venturing upon it will expose themselves to imminent danger...." The effects of Glenfield Tunnel, where some claimed afterwards to have been "nearly smothered", had also been thought of, with a special stop being made near Rothley Brook, near Glenfield, (originally known as Heath Brook, it rising on Bagworth Heath), to allow passengers to

clean themselves ready for the picnic! However, insufficient careful thought seems to have been given to the height of the Tunnel vis-a-vis 'Comet's chimney, for the inaugural train struck the brick arch and the engine emerged at the western end in a less than pristine condition!

After this first 'unreal' day, services settled to three trips per day, with a fare of 4d second class for the relatively short trip to Glenfield, or a massive 1/- for the whole one hour journey to Bagworth. Neither would have been pleasant, however, even on fine days, as any passenger traffic was merely accommodated in open trucks at the rear of the coal trains until 1887! Indeed, no passenger platform was provided at all until 1876, when a very simple affair was supplied adjacent to the Leicester Navigation.

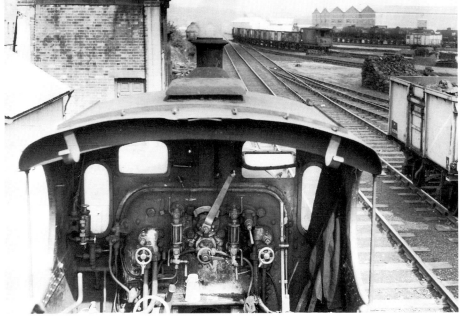

An elevated view of the westwards departure roads from the goods yard, past the water tower, left, as seen from the tender of 58148 on 4 May 1963. Some of the extent of the yard can be judged from this, and one other mainstay of the traffic, the BP oil tanks, can also be seen both straight ahead and to the right. The open nature of the cab can also be seen, together with the strategic placing of Billy can and the hooks right and left for hanging coats. *(R C Riley)*

John Ellis continued his involvement with the railway in the early days, despite his increasing other commitments, but inevitably his close contact lessened, especially as he took an interest in the development of other lines and then eventually became Chairman of the Midland Railway, which, ironically, in August 1845, had swallowed his precious line, to become the oldest constituent of that conglomeration of railways. Interestingly, the wyvern, the heraldic device adopted by the Leicester & Swannington, - it having been part of the standard of the kingdom of Mercia, whose capital Leicester was - was similarly utilised by the new Midland for its shield,

The view towards the city of Leicester, as seen from the neck of the goods yard, with the line to the 'new' passenger platform seen in the foreground and the water tower seen mid-distance just to its left. 58148 shunts mixed 13T and 16T stock on 4 May 1963, preparing for the Duty 51 return to Desford, with the *de rigueur* shunter's pole resting on the buffer beam. The numbered board affixed to the smokebox lamp bracket was to inform signalmen of the workings, in order that the trains could be appropriately routed. The squat building to the left controlled access to the yard. *(R C Riley)*

placing the creature as the crest, overlording ostensibly greater powers of Birmingham, Bristol, Derby, Leeds and Lincoln; and there was even sole use of it on such disparate items as badges and bridges! Was there some Ellis influence here?

Passenger services - and receipts - were never of monumental proportions, (not surprising, in view of the above comments!), although they were obviously considered sufficient to warrant the building of a totally new station at West Bridge, nearer to the then new King Richard's Road to the west of the enlarged goods yard. Opened on 13 March 1893, albeit a simple and unprepossessing affair of single platform and stark brick buildings, (but with a waiting room, hitherto an unknown luxury on the route!), these services dwindled over the years, especially after the line being operated as a branch, following the opening of the 'direct' route from Burton-on-Trent to Leicester for passengers on 1 August 1849 and they finally succumbed to economic realities on 24 September

In the latter years of operation on the branch, there were a number of charter train visits, giving enthusiasts the opportunity of travelling behind the diminutive 2Fs before their demise. Several trips were made by the Leicester Railway Society to the site, two being on 27 April 1957 and 14 June 1958, the party ensconced in a brake van at the rear of the return Saturday goods train to Desford sidings. The first trip was behind 58247 (ex-MR 3176), but in 1958, the honours fell to a rather ancient-looking 58298 (ex-MR 3648), a 1917 5'3" variant of Johnson's MR design and a long-time 'resident' of Leicester (Midland) 15C shed. Seen here, 58298 is about to depart with the 12.15 p.m. run to Desford - the duty here coded '151'. Its more antiquated appearance is seen in the smaller cab-side sheet and roof, and in the original round spectacles; its vintage was confirmed when withdrawn earlier than many of its sisters, in November 1960. Officially the trip ended at Desford, with the participants making their way back to Leicester (London Road) on a service train from Desford station, but on this second trip, the group enjoyed a bonus of being allowed to remain in the brake van for the onward run to Coalville, from where they caught a train back to Leicester. *(Barry Hilton)*

Back to the Deeley-cabbed 58143, and more mixed shunting, with four 13 and 16 tonners being closely watched by the shunter, his pole over his shoulder ready for coupling or fly-shunting. The ground to the left bordered the Navigation, hence the warning of a 10-mph maximum speed (!), and the myriad of points and branches in this quiet backwater looks incredible when viewed from today's vantage point, when once-large and busy yards have been abandoned as superfluous. *(R C Riley)*

1928, when the then remaining passenger services of two trains each way were diverted to the London Road station, in the heart of the city on the Midland Main Line. These two trains were the 8.25 a.m. and 2.08 p.m. to West Bridge from Desford and 1.00 p.m. and 5.30 p.m. return. Thereafter, the line settled to the status of a sleepy backwater, trains slowly trundling coal and oil wagons eastwards to West Bridge wharf by the River, and to the Groby granite quarry siding, with there seeming to be little urgency in any of the operations. Over the years, the

Tunnel made its presence felt, in the way of the restrictions on which locomotives could be used and, with the increase of road carrying capabilities and a need for future investment in both Tunnel maintenance and motive power, plus the working anachronism of manned level crossing points, the end was depressingly inevitable. After trying with modified, more modern steam traction in the early 1960s, the end came with the closure of West Bridge wharf on 18 April 1966, the final train, to clear wagons from the wharf, running on 30 April.

Original motive power, as already seen was 0-4-0 converted to 0-4-2 and nine of the first ten locomotives owned by the line were of this arrangement. Later arrivals mimicked the wheel arrangement, but were larger beasts and these, in turn, were overtaken by more modern (for the day) 0-6-0 types. One of these latter, 'Atlas', was the very first inside cylinder 0-6-0 in the country, being the 'father' of what became the largest single type of locomotive in the country! In later years, stalwarts of the line were ex-Johnson 2F 0-6-0s, and these very nearly saw out the line itself, only being replaced, on withdrawal, a couple of years or so before the final demise, by Standard Class 2 2-6-0s, modified with cut-down cabs. Interestingly, the last three Johnsons on the route were all built in

A later railtour - a joint SLS/MLS 'Leicestershire Railtour' venture - prepares to leave the yard on Saturday, 8 September 1962, with excited heads leaning out of many of the thirteen brake vans, fully intending to squeeze every last drop of experience from the visit. 58148, specially cleaned for the occasion, does the honours. The tour had originated in Manchester and had reached West Bridge via a circuitous route, through the Potteries and then behind a 'Crab' from Nuneaton to Knighton South Junction and on to Desford, where the 2F patiently waited. The tour was at leisurely pace, with the train not reaching West Bridge until early Saturday evening - long after the local Tudor Road residents had been used to seeing a weekend working! *(Horace Gamble)*

Exactly three months prior to the last view, on Saturday, 2 June 1962, 58148 still looks highly presentable and with a good head of steam, as it approaches the neck of the yard on shunting duties, before resuming the 51 Duty to Desford. *(Horace Gamble)*

1876! L & SR passenger stock was never elaborate or numerous, the most superior of the coaches being plain blue painted three compartment affair, with second class as the outside units, with the top quarters open to the elements, and first class in the middle, boxed in but with narrow windows. Wagons were almost exclusively four-wheeled, wooden bodied, with indeterminate colour scheme.

Although unsung for much of its life, the line is now mourned, by both local railway enthusiasts and those historians further afield and very fondly regarded and remembered. Sadly, photographic evidence prior to the last decade of operations is thin on the ground, testament to the lack of regard paid to the line by those photographers travelling widely elsewhere in the country in the earlier years of this century. It still

Its train, a motley collection of mixed-size wood and steel wagons, now marshalled, on 5 May 1962, 58143 gets to grips with the actual efforts needed to shift the load, its smoke adding to the already misty conditions overhanging the nearby Leicester streets and buildings. Note the rather forlorn gas lamp, complete with gauze protection. *(R C Riley)*

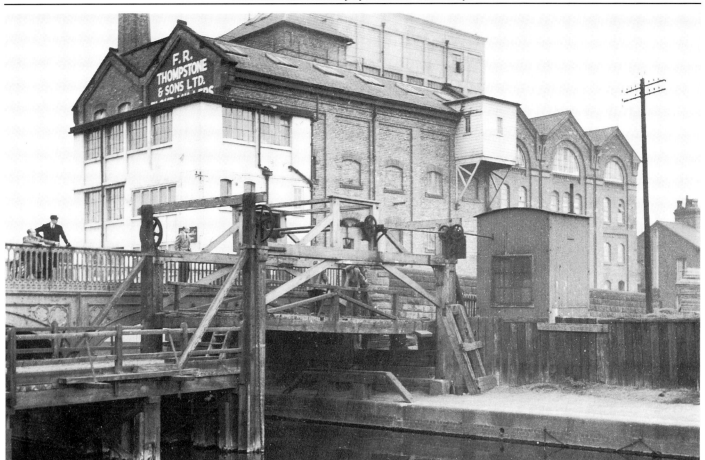

A year after the line had been opened in 1832, an Act of Parliament was obtained to extend the line eastwards across the River Soar, to reach towards the town centre, but the only stretch actually to be built was a 22 chain branch to Soar Lane. This opened in 1834, initially worked by horses and crossed the river on a Robert Stephenson-designed wooden bridge structure that had a portion capable of being raised, to allow any river craft through. This original bridge was replaced by a similar structure in 1847, which in turn received piece-meal 'wear and tear' attention and repair over the ensuing years. After traffic ceased across the bridge, it was kept in a semi-open position, as seen here on 3 May 1960, to allow water traffic underneath and foot traffic over it, by means of a short step ladder. The corrugated hut contained the winding gear. Its vintage is obvious from this view. It was eventually dismantled, initially being re-erected in the Leicester Museum of Technology, but subsequently being moved to Snibston Discovery Park, where it now sits in display, bearing a wagon. *(Barry Hilton)*

retains its place in the annals of railway history, however, and also seems to have been unique in issuing hexagonal bronze tokens to passengers, in lieu of tickets and which were given up at the end of each journey and re-used by the railway; one wonders if there are any surviving in some dark forgotten corner somewhere! On a slightly happier note, in the late 1980s, the Swannington Heritage Trust began work on rescuing something of the glory of the 1-in-17 incline, having restored the Cattle Arch Bridge over the trackbed, planting shrubs and trees for landscaping and planning to rebuild the old engine house, hopefully with the original engine, currently at York Museum, back in situ. Thus part of Leicester's history will have a tangible presence.

Right. Another view of the lifting portion on 3 May 1960, with a woman hurrying into town across it rather than using the Soar Lane road bridge. *(Barry Hilton)*

Above. 4 May 1962 and 58143, devoid of shed plate, seems to be making heavy going of the empty train as it shunts to the neck of the goods yard, judging by the steam that seems to be escaping from too many places for safety! The fireman appears unconcerned with this condition, however, his eyes instead being alert to any sudden movements by the photographer. *(R C Riley)*

Below. The end of the day and 58143 finally leaves the yard and the shunting, on 4 May 1962, taking its mixed train of empty coal and oil wagons past the gardens and impromptu allotments of Stevenson Drive. It is doubtful that Railtrack would allow such proximity today! *(R C Riley)*

Above. A fireman's eye view of the branch's *bette noir*. The portal to Glenfield Tunnel looks appropriately narrow as 58143 approaches on 4 May 1962, with the photographer about to receive a throatful of sulphur! The houses of Dillon Road, on the New Parks Estate, are just visible through the trees. When built, the tunnel was provided with gates, which were locked after each day's services to deter inquisitive animals and locals; a gaunt, flat-roofed cottage sat on the right, where the track straightens, extended in 1874, the occupant of which was charged with the task of gatekeeper. *(R C Riley)*

Below. Finally, a view from the other, Glenfield, end, looking eastwards towards Leicester, with a pinhole of light evidencing the exit just visible in the centre. After closure, there were various schemes mooted to put it to further use, but none came to fruition and it was finally sealed when the local children found it too enticing a place to play! It was sold to Leicester City Council (for £5!), but plans for use as a mushroom farm and nuclear shelter (among other ideas) were abandoned. *(R C Riley)*

A picture that encapsulates all the appeal of steam railways. The throaty roar of LNER B1 61285, bearing the 40E Colwick shed plate, is virtually audible as it leaves Belgrave Road station on 5 August 1962 with the 1X51 Sunday holiday special to Skegness. Sadly, this sight cannot now be repeated, for not only has the B1 gone, but virtually everything in this view has disappeared. The streets, left, have seen remodelling; the station site, after brief occupation by Vic Berry's scrap metal business, has gone, along with the attendant yard, to the developers and road builders; and the old goods warehouse, right, has been swallowed by a Sainsbury's supermarket, after holding out into the 1980s, long after the rest had capitulated. In the latter years, there was a daily goods that trundled gently into and out of the site, but the holiday trains were the real excitement, providing such attractive spectacles as this for local enthusiasts. *(Geoff King)*

14

CHAPTER TWO

GREAT NORTHERN RAILWAY

The station itself, fronting Belgrave Road and proudly announcing the presence of the Great Northern Railway. Seen in the late years of the last century, the road and pavements are wide, the pace of life slower and the confidence of the Railway of its presence in the town is seen from the grand structure and the canopy and wide sweep entrance forecourt, belying the practical reality of the branch to this terminus being a largely sleepy affair for the whole of its life. The main entrance waited under the canopy, with booking hall and ticket office to the right and parcels counter to the left. The station master's office resided the far side, in this view, of the parcels office. Remember the days when billposting was prohibited! *(Leicesters Museums)*

By comparison to West Bridge, the Great Northern Railway branch into Leicester was a very much more grand affair, in length, in operations, in topography and, most noticeably, in the stature of the terminus station buildings.

At the time of its arrival in the town, railways of the area were the exclusive province of the Midland Railway; the West Bridge section, the oldest constituent as seen in the first chapter, had been incorporated into the new Midland Railway Company (still only a year or so old) in August 1845, and the line south from Derbys/Notts, to Campbell Street in Leicester arrived in 1840, the formal opening, from Trent Junction to Leicester being on 4 May. Spurred on by similar desires and enticements to those that drove the Ellis' to the west, the Great Northern Railway had its sights turned onto the ironstone deposits in east Leicestershire, through William Firth, one of its directors. Having learned of the large ironstone reserves in the region of Waltham on the Wolds, he enlisted the support of some of his Yorkshire woollen trade colleagues. These men bought fleece from the area and then, having spun it, proceeded to ship it back to highly

The same view some eighty years later, at the end of 1971, when the site had been bereft of steam for nigh-on a decade but was home to Vic Berry (Metals). This occupation was short-lived, however, as the redevelopment of the road layout and work on a flyover was but a year away, the large attendant roundabout slicing through the right-hand side of this view. Never an attractively designed building, the station here looks positively ugly, especially with the plethora of drainage pipes. The trainshed had gone by this time, as too had the protective front canopy, but the goods warehouse, extreme left, still bore the Great Northern legend. The small boundary wall by the roadside remains, but somehow, even without the canopy, the front forecourt sweep looks distinctly smaller than when horse-drawn carriages would wheel their passengers to the entrance. *(Paul Anderson)*

A detail of the original design still extant in 1972, albeit unrecognised and unloved. The attractively carved gate pillars and the elaborate wrought ironwork still guard what was the entrance to the station cab rank, whilst in the background, the crane stands on what was the main platform. The offices behind the gate became the Foreman's office in 1923 and then Guards' room in the 1930s. Interestingly, amidst all this male-dominated scrap metal area, both bikes parked by the gates are ladies'! *(Paul Anderson)*

successful hosiery factories in Leicester and the availability and facility of rail transport for much of the materials for this trade seemed an excellent idea; hence was born the Newark & Leicester Railway Company, adopted by the GNR in 1871, which, looking at spheres of operation from a vantage point at King's Cross, had plans to put its tentacles into the area, but there were problems with local landowners and other railways who also had desires of their own. Much parliamentary wrangling ensued, expending much energy and expense, before the GNR, perhaps a little unwillingly but in an effort to prevent competitive plans from an alliance of the Midland and Manchester, Sheffield & Lincolnshire Railway, teamed up with the London & North Western Railway, who were spreading eastwards to Peterborough by way of Market Harborough and who were keen to likewise spread

their own territories; the plan being to jointly construct a branch from this latter line northwards, from Welham Junction, some three miles north-east of Market Harborough, to Bottesford, on the borders of Lincolnshire, on the GNR's own line from Nottingham to Sleaford and Boston. Even before Parliamentary sanction was released, progress was not easy, as the powerful Leicestershire fox-hunting gentry were not about to see this iron monster march across their provinces without putting up a fight and as many sat in the House of Lords, their influence should not be underestimated and could not be easily dismissed! The scheme that finally succeeded was the not the first to be presented and even its sanction had a 'penalty', in that the MR was given permission to extend eastwards to Melton Mowbray, from Nottingham, and southwards from Manton, to Kettering, to meet its line from Syston to Peterborough and encroaching on to the proposed GNR territory.

As part of the overall agreement, the GN built branches from the main joint line unaided; Bottesford North Junction-Newark in the north and Marefield Junction-Leicester (Belgrave Road), roughly a third of the way up the joint route north from Welham junction . It is this latter branch that concerns us here and this came late to the railway map, being finally completed and even in part use by 1882, but not opening officially, in

The walls proudly proclaim 'Great Northern Railway Goods Depot' and this was the legend that survived until the structures, including a third equally-large warehouse, added early this century where the dray stands, left, were finally swept away in the mid-1980s. Freight traffic was always the mainstay of the line and all manner of goods were shipped in and out in the early days, much of it onshipped into the town on horse drawn vehicles. Two horses stand by the wagons at the buffer stops, ready for the next load and no doubt they would bring their cargo over the weighbridge, right foreground. *(Leicesters. Museums)*

Although equal facilities originally existed the other side of the fence, left, three platforms were all that were ever practically needed at Belgrave Road, indeed, for much of the station's life, only two were used with any sort of frequency. The single bay, right, more usually provided accommodation for empty and/or stand-by stock. In this view of a wet 22 August 1953, the rake of carriages stretching into the distance was for a holiday train to the East Coast. J11 64438 stands in the central platform with an unidentified train, but is likely to be one of the regular, but unadvertised workmen's trains that ran to John O'Gaunt. Judging by the platform edging, right, much of the glass of the right-hand overall roof has disappeared, letting in the elements. *(H C Casserley/Paul Anderson collection)*

line with the completion of the Belgrave Road terminus, until January 1883. The first public train was on 2 October 1882, when a special excursion ran from the station to Skegness; it is not recorded what the good people of Leicester thought of going to what was often a cold and windswept resort, in October, when the wind would have been bitter if driving in

from the North Sea, but no doubt they entered into the spirit of the enterprise and in the context of the railway's history, it is ironic that both first and last services, although separated by eighty years, should have been to the same destination!

Like the London & Birmingham Railway arriving at Euston, the GNR determined that their entrance to their

new sphere of influence should be as confident and impressive as possible; providing six platforms (a number totally unwarranted it was to prove) for their new terminus station, flush with the main northern road entrance to the expanding town, was certainly testament to those aspirations. Indeed, their ambitions for the whole line seem to have been

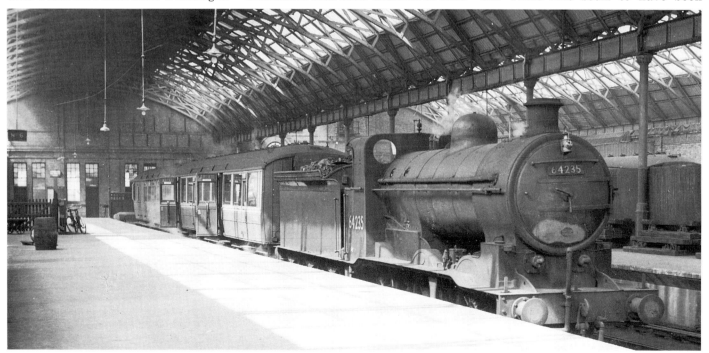

Like the J11 in the last view, Gresley's J6 64235 has suffered from smokebox scorching and looks as if it could do with some Works attention to the smokebox door seal. This view, in the early 1950's, when two trains still ran daily to Grantham, to connect with East Coast route expresses, evidences the station in slightly happier times. Whilst a sleepy depiction, with a bike nonchalantly leaning against the wooden gating, the trainshed looks tidy and well-cared for, with one of Gresley's non-corridor coaches ready for the rush! *(T G Hepburn/Paul Anderson collection)*

When the sun shone, the glass lights in the trainshed led to attractive tracery effects on the inhabitants of the station. The results, captured on Ilford HP3 film at 75th second/F6.3, can be seen on B1 61163 as it stands close to the buffers, having arrived with the 1.52 p.m. ex-Mablethorpe Saturday holiday train of 9 September 1961. On the right, the stock of the 1X38 service to the east waits for its passengers on the morrow. *(Horace Gamble)*

grandiose, if somewhat misguided, with the station buildings along the route, serving what were in truth small hamlets/villages, being on the grand scale and the acreage at Belgrave Road being totally inappropriate for opening and even anticipated traffic.

The LNWR, it seems, derived most from the partnership, gaining fresh and lucrative access to the South Yorks. and

Left. A wonderful, posed photograph of the station and its inhabitants, undated but believed to be 1883. Some of the sheer size and grandeur can be judged and, presumably, the optimism of the Railway in its new venture is reflected in the numbers of staff present. Obviously not all of the 47 bodies pictured here, ignoring the youngsters and the traincrew, are station employees, but the responsibility of covering wages for all those on the books would have been large and a great contributory factor to the financial unviability of the terminus. Note the ornate gas lamps and the extra platforms, right, that became partitioned earlier this century. The locomotive appears to be a Stirling '18 Series' F2 0-4-2. *(Leics. Museums)*

Initially, passenger services ran from Belgrave Road, via the branch, the joint line and then GN's own lines again, to Grantham, where connections could be made for virtually any part of the country then covered by rails. Indeed, at one point, it was faster for travellers from Leicester to York to make use of the morning, 10.30 a.m. 'express' to Grantham - actually likely to be headed by an ageing ex-LNER J2 or J6 0-6-0 with a Gresley non-corridor twin-coach set!, but which was timed to connect with the 'down' 'Flying Scotsman' - than to use the more direct route via the Midland! The lack of any toilet facilities on these trains was a continuing problem and even on the excursions, until the last decade, this was the case, with buckets intended for sandcastles occasionally being used for other purposes! For nigh on fifty years, services settled into a steady routine, there being half-a-dozen trains handling the Grantham service, but by 1950 these had dwindled to just two and then the 'express' was withdrawn on 10 September 1951. In addition, for the pre-War years at the beginning of this century, there was a service to Peterborough, initially launched as four trains per day, travelling by way of Medbourne and the LNWR line, but this was discontinued due to economies needed during the Great War and the service was withdrawn in 1916, never to be reinstated. Having settled into this regular pattern after the War, and continuing through the next conflict and even surviving Nationalisation, harsher economic facts of life began to be felt everywhere in the early 1950's, in a country still trying to recover from the

ravages of Hitler's war and, apart from unadvertised workmen's trains to John o'Gaunt, all regular timetabled passenger trains ceased on 7 December 1953. After this, introduced in response to loud pleas from local authorities, who were concerned at the effect of closure on rural employment, these workmen's trains struggled to retain existence, but with the service being unadvertised, (and one wonders how many workmen would make use of one such, at 1.00 p.m. from Belgrave Road!), patronage was never great and the end of these finally came on 29 April 1957, when Midland Red, the bus company that had grown to serve areas outside of the city boundary, captured the remaining traffic. Then, the only human traffic to be conveyed from the terminus, was that enjoying the annual summer excursion trains to the East Coast.

For many years, it had become tradition for the workers of Leicester, in keeping with many thousands of others from neighbouring East Midlands towns and cities, to take their annual holiday - a maximum of two weeks a year for office staff and one for manual workers in pre-War days - at the holiday resorts of Skegness, Mablethorpe and Sutton-on-Sea and, as these resorts were served themselves by the GNR, it was logical that this company's routes should be used wherever possible and Belgrave Road was an ideal starting and finishing point.

To cope with the normal daily passenger services, plus the solitary one to John o'Gaunt, the workmen's trains and any attention needed to be given to the freight locos, the GN provided a three-road engine shed, situated by the Willow

East Midlands coalfields, whilst the GNR, admittedly accessing its precious iron ore and handling considerable quantities of freight in the area, especially in the earlier days and in the more north-easterly quarter of the county, never reaped the benefits it had sought. The expense of building both joint line and Leicester branch was huge and on the latter, the bleak landscape often brought like weather conditions, leading to continuing heavy expenditure; it was not unknown for locomotives and/or trains to be badly affected and even stuck in snowdrifts! There were hopes that developing resultant traffic would be prolific and profitable (and there was even talk of extending the line westwards, although precisely what route it would have taken through the already built-up area and the enclosed and ancient Leicester Abbey lands close by, converted into the public Abbey Park contemporaneously with the opening of the railway, is unclear), but their hopes and dreams were never to be sufficiently realised.

Some of the partitioning mentioned in the last view can be seen, right, in the form of the white-painted wooden wall, creating a bay platform. Other comparisons with picture, bottom p.18, are a more substantial canopy to the trainshed roof, amended gas lamp design and extension of staging under the right-hand roofing to cover previous trackwork. On the left, the goods siding and acceptance building can be seen, as J6 64257 stands, simmering quietly, before leaving with the 10.30 a.m. train to Grantham. *(J F Clay)*

A rare view into the trainshed of less commonly used platforms 4 and truncated 5, with the latter, right, unusually home to a mixed rake of vans. To the left, coaching stock of the last trip of the day to the seaside sits awaiting the hoards, on 1 September 1962. The very last train ran just eight days later, behind B1 61177 and nowadays such a final journey would be awash with swarms of enthusiasts, gricers and photographers. A few did record the very last day, but seemingly, here, the relevance of this day is largely unremarked. *(Barry Hilton)*

Brook that ran along the southern boundary length of the site. Initially, this had its own allocation and it gave shelter to the likes of Stirling and Ivatt singles and Ivatt Atlantics, as well as all manner of other ancient stock and wheel arrangements, but by Nationalisation this requirement was much depleted and the facility was kept open merely as a servicing point for visiting engines. It finally succumbed to changing circumstances, closing on 11 June 1955, although the buildings lived on long after this date, with some infrastructure, such as the turntable, remaining in use until the end. One claim to fame that is largely unknown, regarding the shed, is that a young 'Bill' Harvey was shedmaster there in his early career, before going on to gain recognition and reverence at Norwich.

Whoops! 170 years of railway progress does not prevent reports of trains failing to stop, so it is no surprise that our forebears had their problems, in days when the learning curve for railway operation could still be steeply upwards. Undated, but presumed to be before the turn of the century, Stirling 2-4-0 No. 639 has well and truly overshot its mark, at the side of the goods warehouse, pushing the very rudimentary buffer stops some way before it. The soft earth seems to have precluded major damage to the locomotive. A gang of navvies, under police supervision, were employed to recover it, but here there seems to be no undue hurry, judging by one man with a shovel! *(Leics. Museums)*

The view from the end of platform 3, looking east, the direction that Colwick's B1 61177 will take with the 9.10 a.m. special to Mablethorpe, on Saturday, 2 September 1961, one year from the end. The condition of the MR coach, right, with patches showing in the roofing felt, was typical of some of the stock that was given to the line for these holiday services. Occasionally there was even non-corridor stock provided, and whilst the trippers were only too pleased to be on their way to (they hoped) sea and sunshine, such non-toilet accommodation did nothing to encourage comfortable patronage! Some Working Timetables included 'Z stops' for non-corridor, longer distance trains - 'stops for lavatory purposes'! - but as far as is known, these holiday excursions were not allocated this luxury. Oil tanks, left distance, evidence some of the extant freight traffic - timber was another important source of income - whilst the ganger saunters lazily towards the station, hammer casually across his shoulder. *(Horace Gamble)*

In the last decade of its daily use, the influx and exodus of hundreds of heaving bodies, suitcases and buckets and spades, to and from the excursions in the main summer holiday weeks, was an exciting one for the younger travellers, whose voices rang and echoed under the huge overall roofing at Belgrave Road and was also one eagerly awaited as a diversion by the local rail enthusiasts. Only three years before closure of passenger traffic, 20,037 holidaymakers were recorded as travelling in 72 trains to the resorts, enduring two-and-a-half hours in crowded compartments, trying to contain excited and increasingly irritable young children and equally irritating luggage! Cameras would be dragged out during the summer weekends by the enthusiasts, to record these arrivals and departures, before very often being put away again during the week, at least as concerns this line. There were few who travelled regularly to watch the isolated engine, either shunting, or arriving or leaving with the increasingly sparse freight traffic mid-week. Inevitably, but perhaps not surprisingly in retrospect, the excursion traffic began to grow slightly fewer in later years, although the trains were still satisfyingly loaded even at the end. At its height, the traffic could be loaded to fourteen fully-loaded coaches and the 'diminutive' ex-GN/LNER 0-6-0s achieved super-human efforts to drag their charges up the prevailing 1-100/120 to near Lowesby, just short of Marefield Junction, a distance of some eight miles. It was only in the last few years that the more appropriate and powerful ex-LNER B1s took charge, but by then it was too late. The motor car was beginning to increasingly make its mark, both in taking the holiday makers to Skegness, etc., but also in encouraging them to investigate pastures new, many further afield; and in addition, after the withdrawal of the regular passenger

For most of its life, the branch to Belgrave Road was graced only with limited motive power, often 'handed down' from other routes after years of use. Certainly glamour was not a usual diet for the route, but one visitation, at least, was made by such an attraction, in the guise of B17 2832 *Belvoir Castle* during the 1930s. In conjunction with a Post Office Exhibition Train, it spent a few days at the terminus, giving the local enthusiasts and travelling public something totally new to look at. The fireman poses for camera, presumably proud of his role and the very presentable-looking charge but certainly not about to live up to the express passenger lamp headcode!. *(Leicesters. Museums)*

The final trip of 1 September 1962 leaves Belgrave Road in bright sunshine for the seaside, with no fond farewell waves from the platform and only a handful of heads peering from the carriage windows. The 'demarcation' between platforms 3 and 4 and the freight side of the complex can well seen in this view, marked out by the signal rodding and the rails from platforms 4 and 5 joining to head towards the freight side of the yard. *(Barry Hilton)*

services, the en-route stations were abandoned to their fate. Although there was not the element of vandalism that is seemingly so rife today, lack of attention did mean that the station buildings began to deteriorate and fall into decay. By the last season, in 1962, they were becoming decidedly suspicious as regards public safety and the trackwork also was suffering. Being a largely freight only

route now for many years, investment was not employed to keep the rails up to standard, with the result that slower speeds had to be introduced. This was not too disastrous for the freights, which had never seemed to be on particularly tight time scales (!), but for the excursions, it became ever more irksome and unsatisfactory. The last year's trains were nominally classed as 'expresses' - and

certainly, from a marketing point of view, this nomenclature was desirable - but as they were now limited to 25 mph on the branch, the name was hardly appropriate!

On the freight side, the ironstone traffic never reached the levels hoped for at the inspiration of the line and, although there was a healthy freight tonnage along the north-south joint line, that on the branch was always more limited, although healthy enough until the post-2nd World War period. Commodities included wood imported from Boston docks, leather for the footwear trade, grain, vegetables and other produce from the rich Lincolnshire and East Anglian soils, and oil, milk and general goods were handled, as well as

Left. Unprepossessing, but nevertheless substantial and attractive, the station signal box is seen during a Leicester Railway Historical Society visit on 20 June 1961. The name giving yet more evidence of the split between passenger and freight requirements, the needs of the former, added to the small goods sidings adjacent, gave rise to the presence of 51 levers to be manned by the signalman. Note the three fire buckets, once ubiquitous throughout the railway system, the chimney for the coal fire in the box, and the plethora of signal rodding and cables, that would give a H&SE Inspector a nightmare today but that were all part and parcel of the past railway scene. There were other visits to Belgrave Road by the Society, including the '25th Anniversary Special' brakevan train of Saturday, 7 November 1964, which ran to West Bridge - two miles by crow, 15 miles by train! *(Barry Hilton)*

coal for the local gasworks and domestic requirements. This coal traffic was given a fillip in 1904, when the town's tramways were electrified and a generating plant was opened in Painter Street, a matter of yards from the station, across Belgrave Road itself. When, during the 1926 General Strike the miners withdrew their labour, the plant was converted to oil-firing and railborne oil fuel was transferred to the tramway's brine tank cars for movement to Painter Street.

Along with the station itself, the GN had provided a large goods warehouse, initially comprising two sheds, but extended to three sometime in this century, and this survived after the closure of the station. Horses queued in the early days, to take the incoming freight out to the waiting customers in and around the city, but these succumbed to motor transport partly before and exclusively after the first World War and the lorries, although much smaller than those seen nowadays and with traffic on Belgrave Road less than since the 1960/70s, would often cause delays to the arterial movement as they turned to gain access to or to leave the warehouse area. Those to Painter Street, especially, being road steam wagons for many years from 1904, caused frequent delays.

Again, as the influence of more widespread road transport was felt, the branch freight dwindled and although the daily goods trip continued after the end of the passenger workings in 1962, this only lasted for two more years. At 5.10 p.m. on 29 May 1964 the final revenue-earning freight left the goods yard at Belgrave Road and climbed the long eight mile climb away from the city for the last time, thus ending eighty-odd years of branch line working. This end to 'through'

Hard by the 'Passenger' signal box and controlled by it, stood this superb Great Northern lattice-post signal gantry, complete with somersault semaphores. Note the smoke guard on the short calling-on arm. Between it and Catherine Street bridge (marked as 'viaduct' on local maps!), is the station water column (one was not provided on or near the platforms), whilst beyond, on 20 June 1961, a visiting enthusiasts' group studies the area between station and the site of the old engine shed. The superb Catherine Street structure was reduced to rubble in 1973. *(Barry Hilton)*

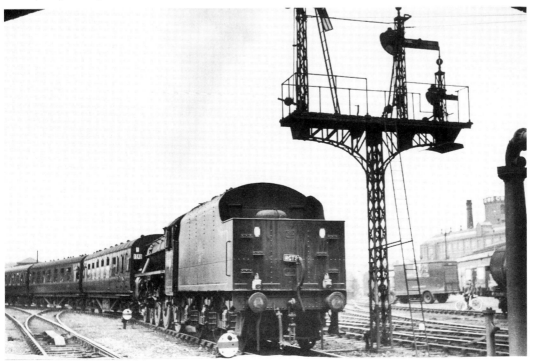

Those signals are seen again, with the outward main in active service, on Saturday, 18 May 1963, as 16A (Nottingham) 'Black Five' 45238 restarts a visiting RCTS 'East Midlands Railtour' out of the station complex. To the right, past the two enthusiasts and their cycles, can be seen something of the still busy goods side of the area. *(Horace Gamble)*

traffic, however, gave a problem to the coal merchant in his yard adjacent to Humberstone station and the petrol depot at Belgrave Road; a solution came from a slightly unexpected direction.

When the original line was being built, a spur was constructed to the Midland main line, which crossed the GN route by overbridge at Forest Road. This was only used for the construction of the route (a decidedly strange arrangement, seeing that the new line was to be 'competitor' of the Midland!), and thereafter was taken out of use and the spur converted into a headshunt from the GN line, although rarely employed; in 1964, when the rest of the through route became redundant, this spur was somewhat improbably reinstated, in order that the coal and petrol traffic could continue and it opened the Monday after the above-mentioned freight. However, the economics of the day - well after Beeching, remember - began to exert their own relentless pressures, both on the railway and with the coal merchant, to the end that this traffic ceased, being lost to road haulage - 1 May 1967 in the case of the coal wharf and 1 January 1969 for the petrol depot - and this last vestige of the line finally closed on 2 April 1969.

Its passing caused little comment locally and certainly there were no campaigns to retain the admittedly rather ugly exterior of the terminus and unlike some railway infrastructure, its bodily presence was not to remain for long. In the 1970s, the Leicester City Corporation needed to look to improving traffic flows on the Belgrave Road, with cars and lorries dramatically increasing in volume and their sights fell upon the station, to give them space to create a huge roundabout and fly-over. Thus, the redundant edifice that had once been that proud terminus building was swept away, together with all the rail area behind it, this latter being redeveloped into a council housing estate and retail park. Catherine Street overbridge was demolished, the road regaining level terrain and all other vestiges of the line were obliterated, with Humberstone station's approach embankment and overbridge likewise being demolished and the coal yard site, near the Uppingham Road given over to small factory units, and even to the extent of filling in the cuttings at the eastern edge of the city boundary, where line dove under the intersection of Uppingham Road and Colchester Road, and building new houses thereon.

As an interesting sideline, the Belgrave Road station area saw two unusual uses during its later years. In 1957, the southside platforms were employed as home to the Leicester & Midland Railway Exhibition, from 19-30 June, where pride of place was given to the preserved ex-MR engines 4-2-2 No. 118 and 2-4-0 No. 158A; entrance to the show being a

Top. **Pre-B1s, many of the longer-distance passenger turns - and, indeed, some of the freights - were handled by Gresley's 1914-designed K2s. On Saturday, 8 August 1959, K2/2 61753 of Colwick snakes under Catherine Street bridge with the 9.10 a.m. holiday train to Mablethorpe, with evidence of another badly fitting smokebox door. Goods wagons lay to the left and right of the train, whilst on the right of this view J6 64213 indulges in some lazy yard shunting with brakevan.** *(Horace Gamble)*

Above. **A superb portrait of an incredibly clean Stirling 2-2-2 No.222. With the afternoon shadows of the shed roof encroaching, the crew pose for the photographer by the coal stage; whether they were the perpetrators of the spit-and-polish, or whether the loco is recently ex-Works is unknown, but the sheer style, elegance and beauty of the Class is obvious from this view.** *(Leics. Museums)*

majestic 6d! And even after the end of services in 1969, it did not disappear without some further use. By the mid-1980s, the name of Vic Berry was big among scrap merchants, both within the city and in railway circles, as he gathered pace in undertaking scrapping of life-expired ex-BR stock, but it is not often appreciated that his first steps towards building this empire were taken at Belgrave Road. The cavernous twin trainsheds were ideal for his operations and he rapidly built up a reputation there, although unhappily for the railway aficionado demolishing some of the platforms and roof structure along the

way. In 1972 he was forced to vacate as the Corporation unfolded their plans, demolished the station area and built that road flyover on part of the site. Initially, the old Goods Shed survived, in private hands and there were suggested uses for it, to retain it, but these came to nought and it too ceased to be, being demolished in late 1985 and subsequently becoming, ignominiously, a supermarket car park! Thus this once proud entrant to the city was gone and it is hard now, even for those of us that knew the line, to remember and visualise what there was and just where it was! Such is the price of progress!

Above. The coal stage can again be seen, left, in a later era, on 24 March 1951, as J1 65007 stands between duties. Note the shed wall behind. This Ivatt Class of 0-6-0s, although small in number, saw many variations in later years, with chimneys and domes in differing sizes and permutations. 65007 appears to be sporting the taller chimney and slightly squatter dome pairing that makes it look very similar to the marginally smaller J5s. Originally 15 engines, 11 survived to BR days, with the last, 65013 going from Hitchin shed in December 1954; 65007, allocated to Belgrave Road sub-shed, succumbed much earlier, in February 1952. *(Alec Ford)*

Below. Heading east away from the immediate confines and hinterland of Belgrave Road station, the line passed under the Ulverscroft Road bridge and then the Midland Main Line. Looking from the former, B1 61092 heads for Forest Road crossing (seen through the rail overbridge), past the allotments, right, on Tuesday, 15 August 1961, with the 6.45 p.m. mixed goods train for Colwick. The mixed nature of the freight traffic on the branch can be judged from the variety of wagons in this consist. Note the long siding to Richards' Phoenix Ironworks, long disused, left, and ahead Humberstone Road Junction signal box perched at the side of the Midland line. *(Horace Gamble)*

Perhaps not surprisingly, the Forest Road crossing was a favourite place for spotters, with the Midland line passing overhead. Despite the backwater nature of the branch, the fact that passenger services in the guise of the holiday trains only had one more year to run, and that the site was remote from the station and amidst factories and housing, the trackwork and environs are incredibly clean and uncluttered with any sort of rubbish or weeds. Despite being manned, it is doubtful whether the same situation would pertain today, when spray paint and vandalism is so rife. The squat, all-wooden Forest Road box is seen on 20 June 1961, during a Leicester Railway Historical Society visit. *(Barry Hilton)*

Just under a year earlier than the previous view, named B1 61247 *Lord Burghley* is watched over the crossing by the Crossing Keeper, in the bright morning sunshine of Sunday, 4 September 1960, as it accelerates away from Leicester with the 9.45 a.m. Skegness holiday train. *(Horace Gamble)*

An elevated view of Forest Road box, taken from the Midland line overbridge, showing the link chord between the two railways. The gradient and line originally constructed when the branch was created, the spur was only used during the building of the route, thereafter being truncated to become a rarely used reverse headshunt from the GN. After closure of the through route, however, there was a problem with servicing the coal merchant at Humberstone station on the GN and the petrol store at Belgrave Road. A solution was found in re-opening this chord immediately after the last through freight had left the area on 29 May 1964. The economics of catering for just these two businesses, however, were such that this new arrangement was relatively short-lived and the whole lot was finally done away with from 2 April 1969. To celebrate and take advantage of the new railtour mileage now available, a Leicester Railway Society tour of Saturday, 7 November 1964 included the spur in its itinerary. Here the stock for the train runs down the gradient behind Standard Class 2 No. 78028. *(Horace Gamble)*

With the newly-laid chord route coming in from the left, the above-mentioned last through freight heads away from Forest Road, past a delightful ex-GN lattice-post somersault signal and a burnt-out ganger's hut. Again a sign of the times, that, despite the bright evening sunshine, there are no enthusiasts/photographers visible on Friday, 29 May 1964, to witness the passing of 61361 with the 5.10 p.m. mixed goods to Colwick, as it begins the 1-in-100 climb to Humberstone. *(Horace Gamble)*

At the other end of that climb from Forest Road, came Humberstone station, actually some way from the actual suburb, and situated on Uppingham Road. The run up to this halt was a short one, as can be judged from this view, as the white factory building behind the train is that seen in the previous view, close to Forest Road box. J6 64230 slows and prepares to stop, with the 1.00 p.m. (SO) Belgrave Road-John O'Gaunt service of 6 October 1956, whilst yet another wonderful somersault signal gives a cautionary right of way to a train in the opposite direction. Note the sand buckets, left, the very fully worded 'Public Warning Not to Trespass' sign, and the missing crossing boards between the nearest tracks. *(Geoff King)*

A vision of what kept the 10/11/12 coach trains in service on the line for so many years. Already with a healthy complement of passengers from the terminus, the incoming 9.20 a.m. Belgrave Road-Skegness train is greeted by a nearly full platform at Humberstone station, on Monday, 7 August 1961. The driver of B1 61142 leans out to watch the spectacle, whilst his charge lets off steam. The holidaymakers no doubt appreciate the bright sunshine, whilst waiting for their train, giving a brighter illumination to the station than the gas lamps behind them ever could! Note the ancient wooden planking of the platform, devoid of the white edging that has graced the opposite side. *(Horace Gamble)*

A classic study in all ways from the halcyon days of steam - of locomotive, freight operation, lineside location and railway infrastructure. With a cautionary go-ahead, the driver of 49444 eases his engine forward, the expression on his face seeming to show some concern at the proximity of the photographer, even though his charge is not about to break any speed records. Like some other ex-L&NWR locomotives, they were unusual among post-Nationalisation classes for not wearing smokebox numbers, but they did display shedplates and this one denotes that the locomotive is part of Market Harborough's (15F) small fleet. Originally designed by Francis William Webb in 1892, as an 0-8-0 derivative of the L&NWR 0-6-0 'Coal Engines', the basic design underwent many metamorphoses over the next forty or so years, finally resulting in the G2A persona seen here. 49444, photographed in August 1959, was built as G2 in August 1922 as L&NWR 2386, being converted to G2A sometime after 1935 and saw use on many parts of the system, finally being withdrawn from Edge Hill (8A) in September 1961. *(Alec Ford)*

CHAPTER THREE

MIDLAND RAILWAY

Built in 1892, to replace the original Campbell Street terminus station, to cope with increasing traffic demands, and to ease through traffic, Leicester's London Road station was a dark place, with the overall trainshed admittedly keeping the travelling public dry, but also retaining the soot and sulphurous emissions from the hundreds of daily train and engine movements. On a bright Sunday, 7 June 1959, 'Jubilee' 45611 *Hong Kong* stands clear of the cover as the late sun picks out the details of the Nottingham-based engine. Seen at 8.05 p.m., the driver looks for the right-of-way to take a 'down' St Pancras-Nottingham express forward, whilst two young spotters discuss some point, perhaps whether it is time they went home! *(Horace Gamble)*

Although by far the largest of the railway companies to operate through Leicestershire, the Midland Railway's conception was very much as a patchwork quilt, rather than some grand scheme of things by one particular proposed line. As we have already seen, the Leicester & Swannington was one constituent and there were common names between this and the emergent MR, but there were other players as well.

The North Midland, tracing its roots back to 1838, was one such, as was the Birmingham & Derby Railway (later with 'Junction' added to its name), but the third of the tripartite and the one affecting us here, was the Midland Counties Railway. Somewhat ironically, in view of subsequent events, the MCR was very much conceived as a consequence of the Leicester & Swannington, with the birth of this latter causing 'fear and loathing' amongst the coal owners of the Nottinghamshire coalfield. As the L&S had been thought of as a way of preventing these same coal tycoons from robbing their

southern counterparts of trade, so the arrival of the L&S turned the tables and a meeting of affected owners was summarily convened in the 'Sun' public house in Eastwood, where it was agreed that a parry to the L&S thrust would be by way of railway from the Erewash Valley to Leicester. William Jessop, credited as being the inventor of the rail chair, was a member of the group, but local finance was severely limited and help was thus sought from a powerful north-west financial coterie known as the Liverpool Party.

Having obtained Incorporation powers through Parliament, the line was built, but not as initially envisaged, as the Erewash Valley was dropped from the plans, the group concentrating instead on developing a route from Derby to Rugby,

A vital piece of railway history so often either overlooked or ignored by photographers, and even some who risked the prosecution, was the 'No Trespassing' notice. Here the message is unequivocal, seen at Knighton North Junction on Saturday, 13 June 1964, forty one years after the Midland Railway ceased to be. *(Horace Gamble)*

There were once seven stations within the city boundaries, serving the various railway companies. On the fast track northern approaches of the Midland main line, the first station encountered was Humberstone Road, a mere 3/4 mile or so from the city centre. The plain 1860-vintage street-level station building gave no hint of the stretching extent of railway hinterland present on the embankment behind it. Local trains stopped here for passengers for the eastern side of the city until 4 March 1968, but expresses steamed straight through and it was a good place for enthusiasts to witness either the speed of those heading south or the exertions of those making their way northwards, climbing the gradient out of London Road station. On Saturday, 28 May 1960, the lowering early evening sun highlights a work-stained Trafford Park (9E) allocated ex-WR 'Britannia' 70017 *Arrow* at the head of the 4.25 p.m. Manchester Central-St Pancras express. Some of the scale of freight operations handled by the sidings, left, can be judged from this view. *(Horace Gamble)*

by way of Leicester, to meet up with the London & Birmingham Railway at Rugby; there was also to be a branch to Nottingham. This latter was the first stage to open, on 4 June 1839, followed by Trent Junction to Leicester on 4 May 1840 and Leicester to Rugby on 1 July 1840. There is some small dispute over the precise date of the second section opening date, but 4 May is the one quoted in local newspapers of the time. Initially, the two 'south facing' railways - the Birmingham & Derby and the Midland Counties - were in direct competition in trying to drive their interests further

There are still pockets of semaphores in the UK, grimly clinging to life, but time was when sights such as this spreading gantry were commonplace. Controlling the northern approach to London Road station, at Beal Street, it here attractively frames Crewe-built 45108 as it approaches the station area with an 'up' parcels train on Saturday, 8 March 1986. Constructed in 1961 and initially allocated to Derby (17A), to handle the Midland main line expresses, the 'Peak' was usurped from this line of duty, along with its sisters, in the early 1980s by the influx of HSTs, finally seeing withdrawal in August 1987. Happily, unlike many of its kin, it escaped cutting and found preservation, as the original numbered D120, at Crewe Heritage Centre. The semaphores evaporated with indecent haste with the commissioning of the Leicester Power Box, built on part of the site of the old engine shed, and the closure of the 'Leicester Gap' on 30 June 1986; and since this view, the old LMS Goods Shed and sidings, seen just ahead of the locomotive, have all been swept away for the ubiquitous retail redevelopment. *(Horace Gamble)*

south, to the main goal of London, but in doing so, they were also driving their finances perilously close to disaster. When the GWR was threatening to invade Birmingham with its broad gauge, it was time for re-appraisal and, thus, George Hudson, by that time influential on the Midland Counties board, proposed an

Top. The gantry and goods shed in the last view are seen again here, behind Engine Shed Sidings signal box and left respectively, as Royston-allocated 8F (known locally as 'Consols') 48169 drifts easily southwards with what appears to be a train of empties, on 11 June 1960. The cramped space into which signal boxes were often squeezed is exampled here by the slightly unusual design, the levers inside and the platform to facilitate window cleaning outside overhanging the track from the Beal Street sidings, on which a 350 HP shunter stands. The alleyway between box and sidings' staff buildings and the bike rack are symptomatic of so many steam yards and engine sheds. What appears to be a spaceship hovering above the train, is the light attachment at the end of a long arm affixed to the box, to enable the signalman to read the numbers of passing locos - for reporting purposes! *(Alec Swain)*

Middle. Leicester was graced with an engine shed from the earliest days, situated close by Campbell Street, but fairly quickly it became restrictive and fresh facilities were constructed across the tracks and to the north of the station. Two roundhouses and a small three-road straight shed were eventually provided at various dates, but again these became unwieldy for smooth daily operation and yet more up-dated facilities were planned, pre-war but not coming to final fruition until 1946. One large, polygonal, 32-road, partly open roundhouse supplanted the three previous structures and the 70' turntable of this can be seen on Saturday, 6 August 1961. Although the loco bays were under cover, the wide central open space gave only limited respite from the elements and for the crew actually turning their engine, none at all. Here, 'Black 5' 44981 of Saltley (21A) is turned prior to working a train back to Birmingham. *(Horace Gamble)*

Bottom. A view from the embankment on the Hutchinson Street side of the shed. This sort of busy view was a constant lure to young enthusiasts and some of the appeal of steam locos is readily apparent from this, as is the very careful planning that was needed to ensure that particular engines were serviced, turned, positioned and ready for their next turns at the appropriate time. Although Leicester Midland (15C) shed had an allocation in excess of 70 at one stage, this shot, with so many resting cheek-by-jowl between duties, was not the norm, it being occasioned by the roundhouse turntable being under repair and therefore temporarily unavailable. On 2 September 1962, the yard contained, among others, home steeds 41225, 41279, 44030, 44231, 42334, 43969, 92120 and 92111, plus 'Britannias' 70010 *Owen Glendower* and 70013 *Oliver Cromwell* (both of 31B March and from Eastern Region turns), 43979 and 48640. The shed closed to steam on 13 June 1966. *(Horace Gamble)*

Top. **Another view of the delights of Leicester Midland yard, this time seen from 'The Birdcage', the prosaic local name for the vantage point overlooking the yard at the end of the Hutchinson Street cul-de-sac. In the late-1950s, the boundary between street and embankment-top was a fence of old sleepers, but such was the proclivity of youngsters for climbing this, to see what was 'on shed', and for them falling off (!), that railings were erected to replace the wood. This meant that inquisitive, excited eyes could espy the yard occupants without hinder. I well remember climbing the sleepers, with some difficulty and in some discomfort as I wore short trousers!, to be greeted with a view of Johnson 0-4-0ST 41518, truly diminutive beside a Stanier 8F. On 4 June 1957, the complement includes 40452, 45267, 42373, 75059 and 44163. The signal box mid-distance is the Engine Shed Box seen previously.** *(Author)*

Below. **The introduction of non-steam motive power to Leicester was slow and insidious at first. The new traction was a novelty, to be viewed with interest (but with horror by some!) alongside locals, regulars and visiting strangers. On 24 October 1959, a lowering sun shines on all of these, throwing shadows of Hillcrest Hospital across the turntable. Brand-new D3785-8 have just arrived, from construction at Derby and make for fascinating comparison of styles with elderly D16/3 62612 (built as LNER 8781 in 1923 and withdrawn one month after this view), a visitor from March. D3785 was officially allocated to 26A Newton Heath as new but came to Leicester nevertheless and stayed being joined shortly afterwards by D3789-91. These seven were renumbered 08618-24 under the 1973 TOPS scheme and of them, old friends 08618 (D3785) and 08621 (D3788) were withdrawn many miles away, from Gateshead (GD) and Landore (LE) depots, in September 1990 and June 1988 respectively. Others seen in 1959 include 44189, 44743 and 44984.** *(Les Wade/Author's collection)*

amalgamation of these two railways plus the North Midland. He was backed in this by John Ellis, of L&S fame and so the Midland was born, being incorporated by this junction of disparates on 10 May 1844. With then in excess of 170 route miles, it was the largest railway undertaking ruled by a single management board.

Inevitably, there were teething problems in this 'marriage' and rationalisation, initially in staff, but close behind in thoughts of operational requirements. No Two people never think exactly the same way and so it was on these three railways. Whilst there was some similarity between the Birmingham & Derby and the Midland Counties, as both favoured small locomotives, the latter the result of the zeal of Edward Bury for four-wheeled engines and the former following the policy set out by their man, Matthew Kirtley, the North Midland favoured much larger engines. Kirtley was chosen to mastermind future progress and he was perhaps an obvious, although not universally popular, choice. He had already packed an immense amount of practical railway experience into his very short life, before he came to the B&DR, having started on the Stockton & Darlington Railway at a mere thirteen years of age and then having fired on the Liverpool & Manchester. He came to the Birmingham & Derby in 1839, as Locomotive Superintendent and was swiftly promoted only two years later, to be Superintendent for the whole railway when the youthful Midland combined the three separate works areas - all incredibly based in Derby - into one undertaking. He was just 28.

The next few years saw rapid expansion by the new Midland, largely under the aegis and ambition of George Hudson and much was in parts of the country well away from our attention, but the proposal to build a line from a junction at Syston, six miles or so to the north of Leicester, to Peterborough, is not without interest, as Hudson had a real fight on his hands with this, faced as he was by Lord Harborough. En-route was Stapleford Park, the country seat of the Lord and his family and he was violently opposed to the proposal, both in its own right but also because of the competition he could see with the Oakham Canal, an undertaking in which he had substantial interest. The Midland's surveyors were met with all manner of obstructions and not a little actual violence, as estate workers and others lined up, pitchforks and other 'local' materials in hand, to prevent progress, but the railway finally won through, although delayed in opening in its entirety until 1848. At this time, the Railway was, under the urging of Hudson, investing and involving itself in all manner of new proposals and it was in danger of running out of both steam

In halcyon days (for spotters) of non-continuous braked freights, more localised trips were most often handled by 0-6-0s of varying sizes, powers and vintage. Progressing from the Johnson and Deeley predecessors, Fowler designed a workhorse that was truly master of its job. His 4F locos and their later post-Grouping compatriots saw many million miles of service and lasted well into the very latest years of steam on BR. Although classified as freight stock, they also saw turns on the slower, stopping passenger trains and on 8 March 1961, 44020 of 15A Wellingborough shed stands under the coal shute, next to Staveley's 48533, in Leicester's yard in the early afternoon sunshine, coaled, watered, serviced and turned after bringing in a Wellingborough-Leicester local; the return working will be handled by the loco later in the afternoon. Externally, it looks in fine condition here, but life lasted a mere eighteen months, being withdrawn from Wellingborough in September 1962. *(Alec Swain)*

This is one of my favourite photographic views of Leicester's railways, the northern end of London Road's Platform 3. Only the engine number gives the game away that we are in post-Nationalisation period, as Holbeck 'Jubilee' 45573 *Newfoundland* eases and prepares to pass under Swain Street bridge on 14 August 1950, with a Leeds-St Pancras express, past an infrastructure hinterland that had changed little over the previous forty/fifty years, including part of the old shed layout, right. Both Leicester 'North' and 'Engine Shed' boxes stand sentinel in the bright late morning sunshine, with, elsewhere, every inch of the view breathing the life and spirit of our glorious railway past. *(Alec Ford)*

The advent of dieselisation on the Midland main line in the late-'50s/early-'60s, including the short-lived Midland Pullman, saw the gradual displacement of 'Jubilees' and their successors ('Scots' and 'Britannias' themselves displaced from an electrified West Coast main line) by Type 4 Co-Co diesels. Universally known as 'Peaks', due to the first ten being named after well-known UK mountains and hills, they eventually assumed the lion's share of express passenger duties right up to 1982, when they were in turn replaced by an insurgence of HSTs. Before this time, however, the earliest examples, especially, began to suffer sidelining from top-link duties and increasingly they saw freight turns. Making an interesting comparison with the last view, late-1959 constructed 44006 (ex-D6) *Whernside*, still with nose-end connecting doors, heads a Sunday 'up' coal train past the 'North' box and into London Road station, on 29 September 1974. Note that although the main gantry behind the box is still extant, so much else of the 1950 view has been lost. *(Horace Gamble)*

(not on its locomotives, but in energy!) and finance, especially in view of Hudson's nefarious monetary dealings. Our friend, Ellis, however, kept an eye on things financial, to the effect that when Hudson was rumbled on other railways and eventually brought down, he (Ellis) managed to maintain both the reputation and financial security of the Midland. This was important, for very shortly thereafter, in 1850, the Railway became part of the first through route to Scotland, somewhat spidery and convoluted by today's standards, being from London Euston to Rugby and thence via Leicester, Leeds, York and the route north to Berwick, but a way through nevertheless. This was to give them a taste for northern possibilities and to lead to the none-too-smooth relations with the LNWR and others on the west side of the country.

As mentioned previously, the 1892-built London Road station was a dark affair, with the overall trainshed cover leading to murky and smoky conditions. Plans were laid in the late-1970s to improve matters and remodelling began in earnest in 1979 and as can be seen from this view, on Saturday, 16 August 1980, the whole image of the place was transformed. With canopies for each platform island now independent and unconnected, there was a much more spacious, open feel; however, this also let in the wind and rain, but you can't have everything! Fortunately, passengers will not have to endure either of these here, as, with work advancing well behind it, a work-stained 45120, still bearing its original split-headcode boxes, pauses with the 1101 St Pancras-Sheffield. Further amendments took place during 1985, with the remodelling of street-level ticket office and access to platforms. *(Gavin Morrison)*

Another view from Swain Street, this time of the station in transition. The new regime is taking shape, extreme left, whilst the old wall, chimneys and canopies of Platform 1 remain. Brush Type 4 47330 arrives with a 'down' express from St Pancras on 18 August 1979, whilst 08609 indulges in shunting of Royal Mail vehicles, the building in the background being local Royal Mail headquarters. Within just a few years, the canopy and short goods platform above the 08, plus the Fox Street carriage sidings on which the shunter is working, will have gone, giving way for a developed car park. *(Tom Heavyside)*

The Midland Counties entrance to the growing town of Leicester was on a gentle north-south arc, skirting the lower slopes of the rising landmasses to the east of the valley coursed by the River Soar and comprised alternating cuttings and embankments, none of too great depth or height, apart from that at Thurmaston, where one of the highest bridges in the region was built to take a green road over the line. The MCR itself, originally promoted in 1836, had decided to place its headquarters in the town and consequently constructed a grand terminus station building in Campbell Street. Although William Flint is generally credited with the design of the neoclassical edifice, railway historians have moved to a belief that in reality it was the work of one of his pupils, William Parsons. The famous architectural historian, Nicholas Pevsner, described it as having six Tuscan columns carrying a pediment, but a visual investigation of photographs of the station would seem to indicate that there are only four such columns, these being flanked by matching pilasters which carried the pediment . Echoing to some extent the magnificence of Euston, it was a substantial building with these four huge pillars forming an entrance that would not have disgraced a Roman Emperor's palace and no doubt much of the drive for this came from William Evans Hutchinson, then a local chemist, but later to become a member of the Board and then Chairman, of the Midland. Originally constructed on a site of nine acres, which local authorities considered to be 'manifestly absurd in extent', but which fairly quickly proved to be restrictive, it initially boasted just one platform, used by 'up' and 'down' trains alike, with crossovers at each end feeding into a loop line. With the opening to Rugby almost immediately and the subsequent opening of the through route

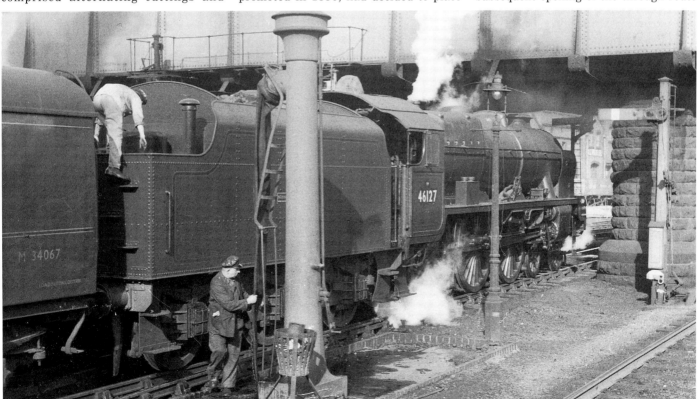

One vital ingredient, but in some ways an Achilles heel, of a steam engine, is the need for water. A locomotive could only travel so far on a given quantity of water and even with the largest size of tender, and despite the provision of water troughs (the nearest to Leicester being at Barrow-upon-Soar), there were still frequent stops throughout the system for 'topping up'. For thirsty steeds having worked in from London or the West Midlands, a water column was provided at the north end of London Roads platform, seen here in this delightfully active view of crew co-operation. A superbly clean 'Royal Scot' 46127 *Old Contemptibles* has worked in with the 10.25 a.m. St Pancras-Manchester Central express of 19 October 1957. Note the brazier, strategically placed to, hopefully, keep the column free of frost during the cold winter months. *(Barry Hilton)*

Campbell Street edifice and built on part of the demolished station layout, but now astradle the main through line, it provided the then much more magnificent abundance of four platforms and was graced with an equally impressive glass-paned train-shed and two signal boxes mid-way along the platforms, designated 'Leicester East' and 'Leicester West'. These complemented those north and south of the new station and remained in use until closure in 1970. There is some thought that the 1869 island platform was altered and extended during this 1892 conversion, forming platforms 3 and 4 at London Road and if this is the case, then they still exist to this day, forming a direct link with those earliest days of the MCR in Leicester - a fact that will be lost on the thousands of passengers using the station annually. The only tangible monument of the Campbell Street beginning, is the existence of the two huge gate posts in Station Street, that now give entrance to a car park.

From 1892, the through lines dissected the body of this new station, with the outer platforms reserved for the 'slower' trains - a situation that still pertains today - and the goods lines were all bunched together on the 'up', eastern side of the station. Passengers for London had been compelled to wait for many years for through trains, but had eventually been able to enjoy this luxury from 1868, when, after much heartache, manoeuvring and inter-Company wrangling with its neighbours, the Midland Railway finally opened its new terminus at St Pancras - 'largest station in the world' - hard by the Great Northern terminus at King's Cross, whose structure the new building dwarfed. Travel time from Leicester, when services had settled into a routine, was slightly in excess of two hours, actually not a bad record, (and certainly a vast improvement on the 4 1/2 hours via Rugby and 10 hours by the fastest horse-drawn coach!), compared to the halving of this by the late-1980s, when one considers the status of motive power then available, the lower average speeds and the generally greater number of stops en-route than is current today.

The above-mentioned wrangling was on two fronts, firstly with the LNWR and then the Great Northern. Virtually from the day that its line to Rugby was opened, giving access to London by connections with trains on the old London & Birmingham Railway, the Leicester traffic was subjected by the London & North Western to inconvenient and often severe delays. With the ever-increasing volume of freight on the Midland, the Company, now under the helm of new Chairman, John Ellis, began looking again at plans, that had earlier faltered, to build an alternative route to the metropolis. Originally given birth by an Act of Parliament in 1847, but subsequently

Two night-time shots of Platform 1. *(Top)* **The precise date is unknown, but believed to be around 1950, as ex-LMS 3-Cylinder Compound 41089 simmers quietly whilst its train is loaded with several trolley-loads of mixed produce, packets and parcels. The trolley, left, standing hard by the Gents(!), contains a motley selection of items, variously secured, including one that boasts 'Locally Produced Eggs. Handle With Care' and is in danger of being squashed! A long-time servant of 15C, 41089 was finally withdrawn in August 1957.** *(Bottom)* **A similar view, slightly further down the platform, a decade or so later. On 11 January 1964, dieselisation has taken over the main services and BRCW Type 2 D5386 waits to haul the 6.48 p.m. mixed train to Ely; to the right, 41228 stands on station pilot duty, surrounded by a truly varied selection of freight wagons and even a Gresley coach. D5386 was one of a large batch of the class allocated to 14A Cricklewood when introduced in 1962, the type being a daily sight in and around Leicester before being transferred to Scotland in the early 1970s for Edinburgh-Glasgow push-pull operation. It saw renumbering to 27103 in April 1974, 27212 in March 1975 (when fitted with ETH capability) and 27066 in January 1982, before finally succumbing to traffic changes on 29 July 1987 at Eastfield. Ironically, it was towed to Leicester for scrapping in Vic Berry's yard, but, happily, the loco escaped the cutter's torch and can now be seen on the North Norfolk Railway.** *(Alec Ford / Mike Mitchell)*

to Peterborough in 1848 and the Burton-on-Trent branch in 1849, the practical working of the station grew ever more complicated and tedious and the facilities of the layout and the terminus building soon began to manifest their deficiencies. A second platform was introduced in 1857, upon the opening of the route to Hitchin and this was then converted to an island arrangement in 1869, following the Bedford-St Pancras extension. The requirement for improvement still

remained, however, and was finally satisfied less than fifty years after the arrival of the railway, with the opening of London Road station, in 1892; designed by the Midland's own architect, Charles Trubshaw, it announced itself to the southern approach road to the town centre in confident fashion, as befitting a new construction and echoing much Victorian building, with an attractive decorated orange-brown terra-cotta facing and proud clock tower. Only yards from the

relinquished in July 1850, the scheme for a line from Leicester to Hitchin, with a connection to the Great Northern taking trains to King's Cross, was revisited. The Leicester & Hitchin Bill enjoyed a smooth run through both Houses of Parliament and received Royal Assent on 4 August 1853, the plan being to run from a junction at Wigston, on the line to Rugby, to Hitchin, by way of Bedford, here crossing

Top. **The present order. Elderly infrastructure still remains (just), cheek-by-jowl with more modern additions, but the passage of time has not been kind to the short goods platform, standing close to the original 1840 Campbell Street station gateposts, which has now been severely truncated and is out of use. The sidings, too, are not in regular use, as can be judged from the weeds growing freely, but at least Platform 1 still operates as a fully-functioning passenger service. On 1 June 1994, BR's 'modern' idea of a comfortable cross-country train, in the guise of two-car Class 158 'Express' DMU 158846 of Norwich Crown Point, prepares to head eastwards as the 0942 Birmingham New Street-Cambridge service.** *(Author)*

Left. **The opposite, i.e. eastern, side of the station to Platform 1 saw home to empty stock sidings and the avoiding lines, enabling freights, especially, to by-pass the heavily used platform roads. Looking south on Sunday, 27 March 1966, there is a bewildering variety of interest, including the 1892 station still intact, ex-MR wooden post signals, a gantry of four delightful 'calling-on' signals, ex-LMS carriages, a lower-quadrant signal (left mid-distance) and a diesel brake tender (left).** *(Horace Gamble)*

Right. **From the south end of this yard, looking back towards the photographer of the last view, 15C-allocated Johnson 1P 0-4-4T 58054 is put into reverse to carry out carriage shunting in 1950. Originally numbered 1341 in MR stock and built with a round Johnson boiler, 58054 has been rebuilt with a Belpaire example, in common with most of her sisters. She was later transferred south to Bedford (15D) shed, from where she was withdrawn in November 1955. Note the advert for Germolene, right, and the name of the Slate Street Boot & Shoe Manufacturers - not to be confused with another outfit with a similar name!** *(John Clay)*

Top. In the heyday of steam, Leicester had an allocation of Stanier 2-6-2Ts, largely for local 'stoppers'. During my two years of travelling to school from Syston to Loughborough in the mid-Fifties, we grew attached to regulars 40146 and 40182, but there were others and London Road was a frequent haunt for some from other sheds. On 20 August 1960, Nuneaton (2B)-allocated 40135 has received the right of way and guards whistle to take a local stopping train to Nuneaton Trent Valley and emerges into the sunlight from the comparative gloom of the trainshed, its healthy exhaust surging skywards. To complete the time-capsule portrait, note the some-what dilapidated state of the station architecture, the adverts for 'Dulux and Du-Lite' and Daily Telegraph's 'Follow Hotspur On the Flat', and the Lambretta parked on Platform 3. *(Barry Hilton)*

Above. A superb vintage view of London Road station. Almost certainly 1892, the exterior of the station is only partially complete but with the 'Departure' gateways finished. The rest of the building saw completion in late 1893, but the station was formally opened by the Mayor, with the inauguration of the booking offices, on 12 June 1892. Minor works continued whilst the station was in service, these finally ending in 1895. To the left is Waterloo Street, a fact endorsed by the legend on the gas street lamp, whilst the horse-drawn tram leisurely makes its way along London Road, towards Granby Street. London Road itself is imposingly wide, considering it is effectively a bridge over the railway, and pedestrians have little fear of injury with only the horse-drawn trams and carts and cycles (and manure in the road!) to contend with. A century later and the view is very different, with the roadway having seen a veritable explosion in traffic and crossing it now needs nerves of steel! Beyond the tram stands St Stephen's Church, built in 1869 and taken down stone by stone in 1893. The MR had bought the site for £6000 and then spent a further £4000 in transferring and erecting the church in DeMontfort Street. The site then became The Wyvern Hotel, later to metamorphose into Shell-BP House, which itself was demolished in the late-1960s to make space for a multi-storey block of flats! Left-distance are signs for Tyler's Boots and Arthur's Boot Palace ('Cheapest & Best'), whilst Leicester Tramway Co. car 13 carries various advertisement hoardings, including for Arthur Pearson & Son of Cheapside ('For Dresses And Velveteens') and 'Rising Sun' Black Lead ('Easiest and Quickest' - presumably for fire grate and stove polishing). *(Leicesters Museums)*

the existing LNWR branch from Bletchley on the level. The construction of the line was dogged with difficulties, not least the terrain and the fact that the work struggled to retain sufficient navvies, and it it did not open until 15 April 1857 (for freight) and 7 May that year for passengers. Although the coming of the line was celebrated by the throngs along its length, the honeymoon period was short, as once again the Midland found that its trains were treated with some contempt and prevarication by its host south of Hitchin. This state of affairs, with GN traffic receiving priority, and the still increasing volume of Midland freight, especially, caused the Midland Board to give thought yet again to their future path into the capital and on 14 October 1862, they took the bold decision to look towards St Pancras. Royal Assent being received in 1863, they began with edging south, but not without adversity and many contracts falling behind schedule, due to more problems with navvies, bad weather, brick shortages and setbacks in acquiring necessary land; but though their progress may have been slow - and expensive - the station finally opened for business (a night mail train from Leeds, arriving without ceremony at 4.15 a.m.) on 1 October 1868.

Back in Leicester, now something of a hub of Midland operations, facilities were needed for the locomotives and, as with Belgrave Road station, an engine shed was sited close-by the passenger station from the earliest time. The meagre facilities provided by the Midland Counties Railway were replaced by the end of the 1840s by a sixteen-road roundhouse, onto which was added a second a decade later, (the two being known as the 'tank roundhouse' and the 'goods roundhouse') and then, in 1893, a three-road straight shed was constructed for express passenger locomotives. Whilst this provided shelter enough, the somewhat ad-hoc building programme led increasingly to problems in the stabling of locomotives, and servicing and preparing them and ensuring they were on the right roads for exit to their trains, became an increasing headache for the shed staff. A more modern roundhouse, to replace all of those on site, was proposed before the First World War, but plans do not necessarily convert into action and it was not until 1946, after the Second World War, that the goal was finally realised! However, even with this new one, coaling facilities were antiquated, to say the least, with engine replenishment undertaken by hand through until September 1954, when a mechanical coaler was commissioned. To relieve the increasing and on-going problems at the shed Post-War, Wigston shed, closed many years previously, was re-opened from 1946 to 1955. This new shed at Leicester, coded 15C under the Nationalisation system, was to have a

For a quarter of a mile or so southwards from London Road track ran in a cutting, alongside Waterloo Street and then Hastings Street. Out of sight of other than inquisitive souls peering over bridge parapets or from upper storey windows in adjacent houses, the line has been captured by the photographer in a privileged position from an entry at the rear of houses. London Road Junction box can be seen in the distance, being left behind by a commendably clean Nottingham-based 'Black 5' 44861 as it heads south under Princess Road bridge with an unidentified early morning holiday special, on 1 August 1953. *(Alec Ford)*

much shorter life than its forebears, being overtaken by progress elsewhere and the decision to end steam on British Railways and it finally closed its doors to steam on 13 June 1966. Somewhat surprisingly, bearing in mind the loss of a need for passenger locomotives, with increasing use of diesel units, and British Rail siting servicing depots many miles from the areas of operation, the depot has survived into the last decade of the Millennium, although the roundhouse buildings were demolished in 1970, (a year after the demolition of that mechanical coaler). The offices are still extant, however, as is the small workshop, but the other remnants of steam days have long disappeared, including the forest of lamp standards and rationalisation of the trackwork to reflect the day-to-day needs of a freight loco stabling point of the late-1990s.

Another 'Black 5', this time heading north. In the early days of London Road, it was operated as an open station, tickets on trains from the south being accounted for at Welford Road station, 3/4 mile or so distant. Its use as such was for a limited period only, however, superseded when London Road erected its own ticket barriers and thereafter it ceased to be a recognised station. The solitary platform, on the 'down' main line remained, however, for many years afterwards and this is the view from its now grassy carpet, as 45234 bursts out of Knighton Tunnel and closes on its destination with a Blackpool-Leicester returning holiday train, on 7 July 1962. This train was common in bringing unusual motive power to Leicester's ex-Midland tracks, the Annesley (16D) engine here being an example. *(Barry Hilton)*

The major difference between the Midland and the Great Central in Leicester lay in the wealth of facilities afforded to goods traffic and the means of getting through the city without obstructing the passage of passenger trains. North of Leicester goods lines were continuous as far as Leeds which meant that southbound goods trains could be diverted away from the main running lines and allowed to filter through London Road, completely isolated from faster moving traffic. A particular difficulty concerning the regulation of goods trains was the fact that many of them called at Leicester for crew relief and for this purpose alone a separate goods line was essential. A goods train sitting on the main line waiting for a guard was the last thing conducive to fluid working.

During my two years travelling daily to school by train, I became used to seeing freight trains nose to tail for what seemed to be the whole length of the journey. At the time, most were handled by Stanier 8Fs, but Garratts were also not uncommon and I never tired of seeing these magnificent beasts, trailing their heavy loads behind them with apparent ease. Mostly they were on the Toton-Brent coal runs, but pictured here, on 10 August 1950, last of the class, 47999 is unusually on the 'up' fast tracks, emerging from the south portal of Knighton Tunnel. It is about to slew westwards around Knighton North Junction, as indicated by the signal, to take the Coalville route, with what looks like a train of power station coal for the nearby Gas Works. Both crew lean from the cab, with the grin on the fireman evidencing pleasure at having his picture taken and, no doubt, temporarily spared the indignity of entering the fixed bunker to bring coal forward by hand! I first saw 47999 in 1955, just in time, as withdrawal came in January 1956. *(Alec Ford)*

An interesting feature of operations in the Leicester area was the fact that many of the mineral services between Toton and the south were diverted away from the district and routed via the 'back road' - leaving the main line at Syston to travel via Melton and Corby, rejoining the main line at Glendon Junction. The advantage of the Melton route was its relative absence of gradients in relation to the switchback nature of the route through Market Harborough and allowed greater loads to be worked. In spite of this there was no absence of activity through London Road; many of the fitted or partially fitted express goods used the route through Leicester as did the traffic to and from Birmingham and that to the LNWR section via Northampton.

Because of the number of yards around London Road there was a considerable

Same place as above, but from the other side of the tracks and the 'pegs' giving a clear road for a holiday excursion to the south coast. Leicester's own Standard 73142 bursts from Knighton Tunnel on 3 August 1957, with a train bound for Brighton, Eastbourne and Hastings. *(Barry Hilton)*

The view south from the edge of Freemen's Common, showing the siting of Knighton North Junction box. In the late-afternoon sunshine, the signalman prepares to lower the arms as Ivatt 2-6-2T 41219 passes and prepares to pass through the Tunnel, heading for its Leicester destination as the 5.35 p.m. ex-Rugby Midland local of Friday, 22 July 1960. Slightly unusually, the allocation of the loco at this time was Northampton, rather than the more usual Rugby motive power, but later 41219 came to 15C and was withdrawn from there in September 1965. *(Horace Gamble)*

amount of trip working in the area, these being engine and men which ran locally to national workings and which could be altered informally at short notice by the district control according to the dictates of traffic. This type of working was distinct from the mainline workings which generally worked as laid down in the timetable.

Travelling south from the 1892 station - 'London Road' until the loss of the city's other stations and the need for this

delineation - the undulating nature of the topography is continued, with the track running first through cutting, then embankment and then on into the 104-yard long Knighton Tunnel. An anachronism immediately north of this tunnel, was a single platform at Welford Road. Built by the London & North Western Railway, this served only those passengers travelling between Nuneaton and Leicester, with trains only calling on Wednesdays and Saturdays for alighting;

it was also used for ticket-collecting purposes, as London Road was built as an open station, but the facilities at this latter were remodelled in the later years of the First World War, precluding this need and it finally closed on 6 February 1918. After this, the basic traffic in and around Leicester was relatively unchanging over the next forty years or so, until, that is, the effects of a growing prosperity in the area manifested itself in the momentum of car ownership.

The line from Coalville met the Midland main line as a triangular junction, giving access to the route from both north and south. With Knighton Tunnel just visible in the distance, 'Black 5' 45209 of Nottingham (16A) has just passed the southern point of the triangle, in line with the gently curving Macaulay Street, left, and is storming southwards over Knighton Fields Road underbridge. Viewed from the balcony of South Junction signal box, the driver relaxes having opened the regulator and given his charge its head, and his cargo of fish gathers speed, on Saturday, 6 March 1965. 45209 went on to be transferred to Carnforth (24L) and lasted until the very last days of steam, being withdrawn in July 1968. *(Horace Gamble)*

Another view from Knighton South Junction box, but on a much less welcoming day. In driving rain, Alsager (5E)'s Brighton-designed Standard 4-6-0 75016 adds to the atmosphere with plenty of smoke, as it heads for Leicester on Saturday, 14 March 1964, with the 10.30 a.m. pick-up goods from Nuneaton. *(Horace Gamble)*

The first line to feel this cold wind of change, was the original 'London' route, to Rugby. After the opening of St Pancras in 1868, the line became a mere branch, generating little freight traffic that could not be equally well carried by road and its raison d'etre relied on passenger receipts, which were never heavy, although for some reason Saturday trains were popular. In 1961, the line was due extensive track renewal, but the costs were not justified by the levels of usage and British Railways proposed closure. The TUCC initially suggested the abandonment of freight and the use of diesel units for passenger services, in an attempt to stave off abandonment, but this was rejected by BR, on the grounds that the Great Central ran a compensating service, (although it was already on the cards that this facility might be withdrawn). There were no grounds of hardship to prevent closure and the end officially came, for both freight and passenger services, on 1 January 1962, although the last trains actually ran two days earlier. The route was not lifted immediately, however, and the sight of long strings of redundant wagons could be seen on the branch for some years afterwards.

Other local passenger services did not fare much better, with the post-Beeching 1960s seeing an end to virtually all such trains and the locomotives that handled them. The Leicester-Burton-on-Trent route became freight only, apart from the odd railtour, with effect from 7 September 1964, when simultaneously, the line was singled; and services northwards from Leicester, through Loughborough, succumbed on 4 March 1968, this leading to the closure of 1860-vintage

Humberstone Road, the only other station within city boundaries on the Midland main line and which had been the northern equivalent to Welford Road, during the open period at London Road. Happily, the buildings from this site still live on. Having lain derelict since closure and with the site needed for redevelopment, BR agreed to sell the listed building for the princely sum of £1 on condition that it was moved elsewhere, and this is what happened, the place being transported brick by brick to Shenton on the burgeoning 'Battlefield Line'. Thus London Road, which now became merely 'Leicester', was served only by north-south and east-west arterial services; London to the north and Birmingham to East Anglia. This, together with the greater standardisation within BR and the all-pervading spread of multiple units and 1980s 'Sprinterisation', has led to some of the carriage sidings being turned over to car parking and other rationalisation of trackwork around the station and its approaches. Alongside this, has been a 'remodelling', (some would say desecration), of the station itself. Reverting to 'open' status, there was complete demolition of the 1892 trainshed buildings, a stripping away, in September 1975, of the overall roofing (which had escaped German bombing raids during the War), and opening of the area to greater light, with modern buildings graced with steel and plastic canopy roofs replacing their predecessors; merely the platforms and street frontage were retained, behind which, the street-level booking hall was completely re-modelled and modernised. Whilst this opening from the previous dark and claustrophobic ambience may be welcomed by some passengers, it is

without the character of the Victorian structure and, also, it does mean that the wind can blow through in greater strength and the elements have an open path to the platforms, so it is somewhat of a mixed blessing.

Of much greater benefit, however, to the travelling public, has been the introduction of the High Speed Trains, with their greater comfort, faster times and impressive reliability. Introduced progressively from 1982, they showed an immediate benefit, with journey loadings rising by 38% between January and April 1983, compared to the same period two years earlier. In line with this investment, the ex-Midland line also saw the introduction of modern signalling. In a pincer movement, approaching Leicester from north and south with colour light signalling replacing semaphores and signal boxes, there remained, by 1983, what became known as the 'Leicester Gap' - an area to be covered by a new powerbox situated on part of the old steam shed, but not yet built, although authorised. This gap became celebrated within railway circles and many photographers travelled to the area to record this 'ancient' signalling while they still could; the reprieve was relatively short-lived, however, the 'Gap', from Glendon Junction to Kegworth, being closed with the new box - then the most modern in the country, containing the technology to cover 179 track miles and dispensing with eighty five jobs - opening on 30 June 1986, in turn signalling the closure of manual boxes at Sileby, Leicester North and South, Wigston, Market Harborough and Kettering. As the decade after that time has progressed, the fortunes of the ex-Midland line have taken an up-turn. The patronage and speed of trains to London have increased; there has been constant talk and calls for electrification to be brought to the city from its present northern limit at Bedford; and there has been investment in restoring passenger services to local lines. Dubbed the 'Ivanhoe Line', and thought up as an antidote to the ever-growing problem of car population and pollution, trains are once again serving stations at Syston, Sileby and Barrow-upon-Soar, on the route to Loughborough, as part of a plan to create a circular route from the latter point by way of Leicester, Burton-on-Trent and Derby. With a combination of demolition of the original station structures, realignment of the track in places and the need for integrating services within existing timetable

The third point of the triangle, away from the main line, was formed by Saffron Lane Junction. In this tranquil view of 17 May 1960, looking west towards Coalville, the layout can clearly be seen, as can the ex-Midland signal gantry. To the left, the houses front Saffron Lane itself and beyond these can be seen the Gas Works complex. *(Barry Hilton)*

constraints, the above villages, although once homes to passenger facilities, now have their new stations built alongside the original freight route of the four track exit northwards from Leicester. The second phase of the plan, westwards towards Burton, aims to re-equip villages along the route with their station amenities and also to create new ones, some within the city boundary for the first time. So, as the end of the century approaches, the gradual and seemingly perpetual decline in rail services in the city has been reversed and the payback of investment has exceeded both requirements and expectations, leading to a more exciting and healthy future prospect.

On the same day as the above, the ancient ex-MR signals, complete with finials, stand blackened with years of sooty deposits, as Leicester's 4F 44519 adds yet more, restarting a train of coal empties for Coalville. *(Barry Hilton)*

A classic case of being in the right place at the right time. The sun emerging bang on cue from behind a bank of cloud, superbly illuminates B17/6 61665 *Leicester City*, about to pass Belgrave & Birstall station on 17 August 1956, heading north on the 'City of Leicester Central Holiday Express' special. The Midland also ran such specials for Leicester's holiday week, when local industry shut down for the period, visiting a different destination each day. B17s were never common sights on the Great Central in BR days and *Leicester City* had been borrowed for the week, to handle these specials - an apposite and boldly imaginative move by whoever was in Control. I missed all of these runs and so determined to obtain one of the engine's name plates when withdrawn. When the event occurred - from Yarmouth (South Town) (32D) shed in April 1959 - I was offered one of the two plates, including coloured splasher with football, by BR for £13.10.0, but sadly father would not lend me the requisite sum! - it was subsequently purchased by The Leicester Railway Society (without football) for £5. Today, that same full plate would fetch in the region of £30,000 and I have had to satisfy myself with a scaled down replica. In the 1990s this train would be at the preserved Great Central Railway's Leicester North platform, with the station entrance being roughly adjacent to the site of the signal above the second coach. Sadly, the original station, on whose platform the photographer is standing, and the period signal box, left, are no more, the former a victim of vandals in the 1970s. *(Geoff King)*

CHAPTER FOUR

THE GREAT CENTRAL RAILWAY

Belgrave & Birstall station in happier and sylvan times. In the morning sunshine of 24 April 1957, a remarkably clean K3, 61975 of Annesley, lazily passes the station with a southbound train of delightful variety. What can be seen of the station itself evidences that much care and attention is lavished by the staff and it is a fine example of a GC island structure. Entrance was gained by steep covered stairs from the ornate edifice fronting appropriately-named Station Road, with the village beginning where footpath met bridge, on the extreme right of picture; the open space beyond the fencing across the tracks, belongs to Birstall Golf Club. For many years, my maternal grandfather had an allotment here and when I visited (and later cultivated) the plot I would be constantly rushing to this very vantage point, just to watch the trains go by. *(Geoff King)*

U ntil the proposal and final sanction by Government for the building of the Channel Tunnel Rail Link, to create a 'fast-track' route to the Tunnel and on into Europe, the Great Central Railway, a century earlier, was the last main line built in this country and it is ironic that the driving force behind the conception of the GCR, was a plan to link the England with its Continental neighbours

Known throughout its life as 'The Last Main Line', this grand sounding venture started life as a plan to extend the Manchester, Sheffield & Lincolnshire Railway southwards, with then an eye on extending further to the south coast and a tunnel under the English Channel and was, consequently, engineered to the continental loading gauge. The eventual grand scheme was to run through trains from Manchester (and possibly even Blackpool) to Paris, skirting around London, but having connections with the capital; not a lot seems to have changed over the intervening ninety or so years

The MSLR had itself grown piecemeal, with origins tracing back to 1836 and the Sheffield, Ashton & Manchester Railway, but it had developed to become a thriving and important cross-country railway,

When the station was being built, there were no allotments nor yet houses close by. The town/county boundary ran through the platforms (just to the south of the entrance and steps) and the resultant name given to the site by the GC was an amalgam of village and the nearby area of Leicester. With the lion's share of the site being within the urban jurisdiction, Belgrave was given title preference. Although the GCR opened to Marylebone in 1899, construction had been ongoing for a number of years previously and this is the view in late-1896/early 1897 with the outline of both bridge and station rapidly taking shape. *(Leics. Museums)*

Top left. Some seventy years or so from construction and services have ended. After the end of through trains to London, in September 1966, a diesel multiple unit service was introduced between Rugby and Nottingham, with tickets being sold on the trains and the intervening stations left as unmanned halts. Seen in the summer of 1969, only a couple of months on from the end of these trains on 5 May, weeds are already reclaiming territory, but, remarkably in view that there has not been staff here since the withdrawal of stopping services on 4 March 1963, there is no apparent sign of vandalism - a real sign of the times, but one that would change swiftly within two years! Demolition finally came in 1982. Just past the end of the platform can be seen the brick abutment that marks the site of the signal box, and, left, are the afore-mentioned allotments. When I saw this photograph, I could hardly believe my eyes, as the gardener, assiduously applying fork to soil, is none other than your author! *(Paul Anderson)*

Middle left. During the construction of the Great Central, Leicester photographer S W A Newton embarked on a self-imposed crusade to capture as much of the work and progress as possible. He has left us with a treasure chest of images, covering all aspects of the task, including demolition as well as building, works tracks as well as main line, industrial locos, important addresses and the labour force tasked carrying out the often back-breaking work. Many of the latter were skilled in their trades and two of these, burly blacksmiths, are captured by Newton in their makeshift forge at Mowmacre Hill, immediately to the south of Belgrave & Birstall station. *(Leics. Museums)*

Bottom left. As constructed, the railway was carried into Leicester on a mile-long elevation, comprising a series of embankments and bridges as it approached the town from Abbey Lane sidings. There were six crossings of River Soar and the canal. Many slum dwellings were demolished in the process, generating not a little opposition, but this had the ancillary benefit of opening out some of the over-densely populated (and infested) areas on the western fringe of the town centre, (although the Railway was forced to build 300 new houses to partly replace some of those demolished!). Seen in the late-1890s and looking from the King Richard's Road direction, girders for the bridge over St Augustine Street are raised into position, with two brave (foolhardy?) navvies precariously perched on one of them. The gang in the foreground concentrate on their winch, whilst policeman and bowler hatted gentleman by him - and no doubt the crowd - watch these two acrobats. The event was obviously a great attraction and may have even been a special occasion, as many of the throng spilling from West Bridge are attired in bowlers, white collars and ties, and smart looking coats. A Roman pavement was discovered during demolition and fortunately this was preserved. *(Leicesters Museums)*

A graphic display of what can happen when a locomotive becomes too inquisitive about its surroundings! The date is the morning of Sunday, 25 September 1949, some twelve hours since O4 63862 leapt through the retaining wall on the northern viaduct approach to Leicester central station, bringing mayhem and rubble to the back yard of a fishing tackle shop! The O4 had left Woodford Halse the previous evening at the head of an empty coal train for Langwith, arriving at Leicester around 8.45 p.m., having run north as usual behind B1-hauled 6.55 p.m. Woodford-Leicester stopper. Unfortunately, circumstances conspired against the normal routine of B1 having left its train in the station and being well on the way to the Central shed by the time the freight arrived and on this evening, the latter, nearly at line speed, and B1 collided just past Leicester North box. Fortunately, the B1 (61108) stayed (just) on the viaduct, but the O4 plunged 25ft. earthwards. The engine is seen severely damaged beneath bricks and vertically-perched tender, the load of this latter having been shot through a storeroom at the rear of the shop; several bodies peer at the wreckage, but happily there were no fatalities. The full bizarre story, eloquently told by Paul Anderson, can be read in the February 1996 issue of *BRILL*. *(Leicesters Museums)*

drawing a steel line across the Pennines, linking the Lancashire and Yorkshire coalfields and the coastal resorts and outlets of the Great Grimsby and New Holland areas. Its great drawback, however, was that its operations were thus concentrated in an admittedly prosperous and vibrant industrial corridor, but it had no route to London and any traffic for this destination was perforce to travel via the courtesies of rival Companies. Not surprisingly, the Railway's management and more specifically its Chairman, Edward Watkin, was neither happy nor relaxed about this state of affairs and they looked to expansion and finding ways south, by forging relations with competitors if necessary. An early plan in 1873 to make alliance with the Midland for a new railway came to nothing, and several other similar schemes over the next twenty years or so all collapsed in similar fashion. Never daunted, however, and keeping his sights firmly on the goal, Watkin, also Chairman of the Metropolitan and the South Eastern Railways, pursued his options with an energy belying his seventy-odd years and eventually Parliamentary sanction was given, in 1893, for an independent line, to run from Annesley, some nine miles north of Nottingham, to Quainton Road in Buckinghamshire, where running powers would be agreed over the Metropolitan Railway to Finchley Road, and thence again on its own tracks into a new terminus at Marylebone. This latter part of the plan caused friction with the Metropolitan, as they had hoped that Baker Street would be chosen as the terminus and, in turn, this conflict led to delays in the opening of the GCR and the creation of an alliance with the GWR, for running powers over the lines through High Wycombe, giving access to Marylebone that way, but not until 1905/6. Another potential stumbling block, was the passage of the line directly underneath Lords Cricket Ground, in St John's Wood. Initially vehemently opposed by supporters of the hallowed turf, the Marylebone Cricket Club (MCC) wrung beneficial financial terms from the

Just how the railway carved its line through this area is graphically displayed here, with the view looking north from the signal gantry at the northern end of Central station; again, sadly, services have ceased and nature is colonising. To the left is Northgate Street, which despite its appearance here, was an extremely busy arterial exit to the west from the town. The point of 63862's leap is now marked by the railing fence, left. *(Paul Anderson)*

For the building of the Great Central through the town, various offices were established in Leicester. 25 Gallowtree Gate was bought by the railway, initially as a contractor's office, but thereafter, occupied by Messrs Dean & Dawson to act as agents, it covering a multitude of operations. In the early years of this century, it advertises itself ready for: receiving parcels, passenger booking and enquiries, tourist and excursion information, and, presumably sitting happily with Chairman Watkins' original plans of Channel Tunnel traffic to the rest of Europe, the issue of tickets "to all parts of the Continent". A very proud boast for the period - and no computers controlling affairs! Presumably, business was sufficiently successful, as Dean & Dawson went on to become a household name in the town as travel agents. *(Leics. Museums)*

Railway, as well as securing assurances regarding the non-disturbance of play (!), and all were placated, with the first sod being cut in nearby Alpha Road on November 13, 1894. Final opening of the more direct route to the metropolis was on 15 March 1899, but not to tumultuous reception, as only fourteen people travelled on the second train, the 9.15 a.m. express northwards - the first, with just four souls aboard, had departed at 5.15 a.m.!

The overall scheme was bold and in keeping with the confidence and pride of the late-Victorian age, but finances were

One of the delights of the GC was never quite knowing what would appear next, either on freight or passenger turns. Post-Nationalisation, the 'crack' express duties, such as 'The South Yorkshireman' or 'Master Cutler', although rostered for a B1 south of Sheffield, were often handled by Gresley's superb A3 Pacifics, especially 60059 *Tracery*, 60102 *Sir Frederick Banbury*, 60104 *Solario* and 60111 *Enterprise*, with B1s holding the ring with the slightly slower services. 'The South Yorkshireman' began on 31 May 1948, (10 a.m. from Bradford Exchange), becoming the first named train to be introduced by the then still very young British Railways. Later, and as control over the GC route passed to the Midland Region of BR, V2s, B1s and Stanier 'Black 5s' took the lion's share, but all manner of locomotives could turn up. It was always a delight, however, to witness K3s at the helm, with their massive-looking boilers giving them a truly impressive persona. On Friday, 5 May 1961, Immingham (40B)'s 61970 seems over-powered as it passes over Soar Lane and arrives at Central station, its destination, with the 4.15 p.m. local stopper from Nottingham (Victoria). The gantry of the view at the foot of p.47 is seen above the first coach, with the controlling North signal box to the left. The girder carries the line over Northgate Street. *(Horace Gamble)*

not unlimited. The costs of initially purchasing the required land were massive, as were the engineering feats needed to make the line as fast running as possible, without too many steep gradients or adverse curvatures. Indeed, the outlay on these alone drained the undertaking so much that there was barely enough left to expend on the rolling stock and the locomotives desired to haul the new services were required to be obtained by way of hire purchase. What this did provide, however, was one of the finest main lines built for the country's railways and one with great potential for fast running and speedy services; it is unfortunate, therefore, that, coming late, the line was forced to run through much rural landscape, away from centres of great population and thus with little real prospect of attracting substantial

Top. With the railway entering the town on an elevated plane, street level entrance, forecourt and ticket office were divorced from the platforms, down steps and along a dim subterranean passage. Originally built with an ornate parapet of Flemish-style pinnacles and central clock tower, the public, street facade never quite had the style and grandeur of either Belgrave Road or London Road, due to a mixture of changing Victorian fashions and tight budgetary purse strings, but it was solid enough. This sheer solidity has assisted its survival through to the 1990s, standing guard to the motor businesses operating from former forecourt and offices. In 1970, the gates are closed, evidencing cessation of services, but the BR signs still proclaim its prior status, one above the main gate and one at the far end of the building. The Austin 1100, Ford Corsair and Reliant Robin all add period flavour. *(Paul Anderson)*

Middle. Another piece of architecture that has survived the dereliction of the railway and the ravages of time, is the ex-Parcels Offices entrance, at the southern end of the station frontage. The ex-GC offices within are also still extant, occupied by A & P Autos, the motor business owning the lorry seen through the gates. As a link with the past, Horace Gamble's mother worked in these offices as a wages clerk, prior to her marriage in 1921. *(Paul Anderson)*

Bottom. Ticket office staff briefly pause from their duties, to pose for this delightfully evocative portrait of their domain. Judging by the number of Edmundson tickets neatly positioned in the racks, there are a myriad destinations anticipated and no doubt each ticket clerk was required to learn them all. The five officials, all in varying styles of uniform, are blessed with plenty of space in which to work and their drawers, ledgers, coats and hats, high stool desks and ink wells all speak of the period. Interestingly, although the office was obviously originally furnished with gas lamps, electricity has been introduced, but the light arrangement over the desks appears somewhat impromptu. *(Leics. Museums)*

49

A view of the southern end of the Central station during construction. The massive hydraulic buffers in the bays await completion, whilst mid-way up the platforms, contractors' wagons stand to take away spoil, having brought in materials. Two of the water towers provided at the southern end can be seen in the mist and the shape of the covering canopies is becoming clear; but it will still be some time before passengers are vouchsafed this view. Excavations to lay the foundations of the station uncovered many valuable archaeological finds, one of which, a tessellated Roman pavement, was preserved *in situ* in a large room underneath the platforms. *(Leics. Museums)*

passenger revenue. Freight traffic was the line's salvation and, indeed, its bread-and-butter throughout its life, but even was this was to suffer, through the sometimes petty politics of competing railways and when amalgamations of areas became the norm after Nationalisation, old rivalries and grudges surfaced to wield first a scalpel and then a butcher's knife to the route and its services. When opened in the last years of Victoria's reign, however, it strode forth in confident guise, as if determined to live up to its new 'Great Central' name.

Whereas earlier railways had built their lines very much in response to existing topography, using prevailing features of the landscape wherever possible to facilitate ease of access, the GCR seemed more to have drawn a line on the map between two points and built as close to that line as possible. Hence there were impressive embankments and deep cuttings cheek-by-jowl, as the railway strode defiantly on its way, seemingly impervious to the results of the ice-age, but determined to create a race track for its locomotives. With no gradient more than 1-in-176, it certainly achieved this ambition, allowing its handsome and graceful engines to speed to best advantage. They were helped, of course, ironically, by coming late to the scene, as they were able to employ all manner of steam cranes, contractors' locomotives

A classic, oft-seen view, but still worthy of repetition. Judging by the intending passengers, the time is shortly before 3 p.m. on Saturday, 18 October 1901 and the ticket examiner, proudly wearing his GCR cap and his title on the collar of his jacket, clutches his punch as he poses with the train indicator. Local trains, from north and south bays, are signed for Nottingham and Brackley, whilst expresses are due in an hour or so for Marylebone and Manchester. Although there is no indication, it is presumed that travellers to Huddersfield, Halifax and Bradford, will reach their destinations by changing at Sheffield rather than by enjoying through coaches. The newspaper hoardings behind the seat provide fascinating reading, referring to the debate on The Education Bill in parliament, a Parisian divorce hoax (!), Joseph Chamberlain MP and Boer Generals in 'official contradiction', reference to Lord Kitchener, and report of King Edward VII's visit to the City (presumably London, as Leicester was still just a town at this time). *(Leics. Museums)*

and other refinements that had not been the luxury of their forebears. The amount shifted by these means daily was prodigious and far in advance of what had been achieved by the mere manual labour by previous railway navvies.

Due to the costs of construction and the high price of land, acreage purchased and developed by the railway was kept to as much of a minimum as possible, within the confines of the grand scheme, and this led to most of the stations being constructed as islands, where the fast running tracks diverged slightly from the 'straight' to accommodate the obstruction. Many of the stations were built in cuttings, reflecting the undulating nature of the area and the entrances were both grand staircase entries to this new world, with the exterior road buildings having a singular appearance and, also, potentially dangerous affairs, as the steepness of the steps was quite daunting. Leicester Central, unlike its neighbours on the line, was the opposite, being built high above street level on a massive man-made embankment. Here, the entrance was by way of upwards stairs leading up from a

In the early days of the GCR, restaurant car facilities were provided for those fortunate enough to afford them, but on-train water capacities were limited, necessitating stops at strategic points for topping up. In early Edwardian days, a porter stands on Central station with water tank ready to replenish the on-board container of a Marylebone-bound express. Behind, the two ladies (mother and daughter?) seem delighted to somewhat coquettishly sneak into the picture. *(Leics. Museums)*

Leicester Central boasted superb Refreshment Rooms, not unlike that depicted in *Brief Encounter*. During my first days of employ by Barclays Bank in the city, I would join friends on the station for lunchtime sandwiches and a pint of Double Diamond. The GCR provided furnishings and cutlery, plates, etc., with their initials proudly emblazoned and these could still be found right up to the end of facilities on the station. The eastern entrance to the Rooms can be seen, left, as D11/1 'Large Director' 62661 *Gerard Powys Dewhurst*, of Staveley GC (41H) shed, waits to return north with the 8.55 p.m. stopper to Nottingham Victoria of Saturday, 13 June 1959. Whilst commonplace pre-war, 'Directors' had been absent from the GC in Leicester until 1958/9, when a rostered turn was introduced for an early evening run to Leicester from Nottingham and almost immediate return; the sight of this locomotive variety was Manna for local spotters and photographers alike. Originally GC Class 11F No. 507, built at Gorton in 1920, this engine saw exactly 40 years service, being withdrawn from Staveley in December 1960. *(Horace Gamble)*

In common with other interchange stations, such as Oxford and Banbury, where trains to and from other regions used the route, Leicester Central saw a bewildering array of locomotive types, of all regions, including Western and Southern. Either of these could be seen on the Bournemouth-York cross-country trains, changing engines here, with the visiting motive power not routinely venturing north of the station. On 16 August 1958, 5916 *Trinity Hall* of Oxley (84B) and 4970 *Sketty Hall* from more distant Taunton (83B) - neither of which was a regular visitor to Leicester - make use of the station turntable and watering facility overlooking Great Central Street and Friar's Causeway. These facilities were provided here as the engine shed was some 1 1/2 miles south, accessed from the main line and running to and from the shed for servicing would have severely disrupted traffic flow. On the left is a delightful variety of motive power, in the guise of K2/2 2-6-0 61753 of Colwick (38A). *(Barry Hilton)*

In later years, one of the regular and now fondly remembered sights on the GC was Standard 9Fs on the prosaically-named 'Windcutter' coal trains. Unremarkable and largely unremarked at the time, their steady rhythm, either plodding manfully up gradients, or racing down them, were nevertheless an integral part of the scene and a large money earner for the line; they even occasionally substituted with great aplomb on passenger turns. Here, at the southern end of Central station in April 1962, 92091 has neither freight nor passenger duties, running light engine through the station to return to Annesley shed. *(Alec Ford)*

cavernous passage from the street and ticket office. There was also the luxury of a hydraulic lift, but this seems to have had relatively little use and a correspondingly short life. The viaduct, which had occasioned the demolishing or rebuilding of some 300 (admittedly slum) dwellings in the late 1890s - in many ways similar to the devastation wrought in Nottingham in a poorer part of the town, in Watkin's desperate attempts in both places to be close to the centre of town - swept in a gentle arc north to south as it entered the city and ran for over a mile. Ninety seven blue brick arches proudly carried it across the surrounding valley, with eleven plate and two impressive bowstring lattice girder bridges spanning the various streets and roads it met on its way and three other lattice girders carrying it over the River Soar and canal, close to the terminus facilities of the Leicester & Swannington Railway at West Bridge, as seen in Chapter 1.

Of all the stations on the whole route, Leicester Central was probably the most palatial, extrovert and magnificent of the Great Central structures, (Nottingham Victoria, opened on 24 May 1900, although greater in area, was a joint station with the GNR), and its street entrance facade was built to match. With three wide

Long before German Federal-type smoke deflectors were fitted to the class, Leicester Central shed (38C)'s own A3 60102 *Sir Frederick Banbury*, with the express code headlamps duly in place, makes a spirited departure from the station just before Midday on 14 August 1950, with a Manchester-Marylebone train. Note the ex-GC lower quadrant starter signal, unusual in avoiding being converted to upper quadrant before being replaced by colour lights. Built in July 1922, the second of two prototype Gresley A1 Pacifics for the LNER's main line out of King's Cross, but later having been a regular on the top link expresses over the GC for many years, *Sir Frederick Banbury* was transferred away in the mid-'50s, finally ending up at King's Cross Top Shed (34A), from where it was withdrawn in November 1961. This vantage point, at the end of Talbot Lane cul-de-sac, although reached courtesy a stout wooden door and trespassing, was a favourite with spotters - unfortunately, it was also popular with the Transport Police! *(Alec Ford)*

entrance gateways, each flanked by large windows, it was crowned by a parapet of nine ornate gables and a somewhat out-of-proportion clock tower capped by an onion-shaped cupola. Finished in orange bricks, this attractive frontage led into a courtyard, fully glass-roofed, and an airy booking hall, before that dingy subway passage took intending passengers to the platform steps. During excavation of foundations for the station, many archaeological discoveries were made, not least a tessellated pavement from a Roman building and this was preserved *in situ* in a large hall beneath the

platforms. Once more in daylight, intending passengers had a choice of six platforms - one each for 'up' and 'down' through trains and bays at both north and south ends of the island arrangement, each with two tracks - far in excess of the facilities at Midland's London Road, but with far fewer services to be handled from them! On the platforms, comfort facilities were extensive for the period, even stretching to both restaurant and dining rooms (!), decorated a mixture of dark woodwork and brown and green tiles. These gave countless hundreds of travellers fine fare in sumptuous

surroundings, and even post-Nationalisation, when the restaurant closed at the end of 1951, the original fittings were still extant and plates, cutlery and crockery bearing the coat of arms of the GCR were still in use

In a depressed part of the town of Leicester when it arrived, the station's external appearance certainly enhanced the surroundings, but the area, despite being only half a mile of so from the centre (and slightly closer than London Road to this extremely busy area of activity), remained unfashionable and today, a century later, it is still the same.

Almost immediately from opening, the line was very busy and the variety of traffic on the route was matched by the locomotives employed to haul it. Whilst Annesley and Woodford engine sheds were most largely populated by freight engines, reflecting the nature of the cross-country traffic that was still there from before the opening of the 'London Extension', and Gorton and Neasden (at the Manchester and London extremes of the system) coped with both freight and passenger locomotives, it was perhaps Leicester Central shed that saw the widest variety. Being a convenient 'half-way house', it was often to see use as a staging post, where locomotives would change - particularly after the last war -whilst the introduction of cross-Railway services, such as the York-Bournemouth expresses, or the Annesley coal, Scunthorpe steel and Immingham fish trains to Wales and the west, brought the occasional sight of other Railways/regions engines. Indeed, the Oxford-Leicester service, introduced in 1900 and operated by the GWR across the 'spur' from its own line at Banbury, to Culworth Junction on the GCR, daily brought engines of this company into the Central heartland. Mostly these would be turned on the station turntable, prior to being watered and readied for the return trip to their own sphere of operation, but on occasions, they would repair to the shed, where they would provide excited viewing for those brave enough to enter the shed confines from the canal path at the rear. Also, with the weight of fish traffic - prior to the First World War, over ninety percent of fish landings at Grimsby were sent south by rail - it was not unusual to see an Immingham-allocated loco in for some attention.

Over the years, it gave home (amongst others) to a few of Robinson's handsome 4-6-0s, C4 4-4-2s, B17 'Sandringhams', A3s (including 60103 'Flying Scotsman' from June 1950 to November 1953), B1s, 'Black Fives', 'Jubilees' and even 'Royal Scots', as well as a wide variety of 'lesser' fare. During the War, all manner of ex-LNER could be seen, including Q5 and Q6 0-8-0s, B15 and B16 4-6-0s, O4 2-8-0s and even the USATC S160s often repaired to the shed

As stated previously, the GC was carried through Leicester on a mixture of embankment and girder bridge; this is the one immediately to the south of Central station, carrying the railway across the Leicester Navigation arm of the Grand Union Canal. On 6 August 1966, with just a month to go before the end of through trains to London, 'Black 5' 44848 restarts a Nottingham-Marylebone semi-fast (8.54 a.m. off Leicester), passing under the impressive gantry controlling the southern entrance to the station. *(Horace Gamble)*

The next bridge south was, officially, Duns Lane bridge, but, set at the confluence of Braunstone Gate and The Newarke, it was always known locally as Braunstone Gate bridge. In this early summer's view of 1898, the structure is virtually complete and no doubt would have been something of an attraction. The two ladies taking a genteel stroll, with parasol to guard against the midday sun, have no doubt just come from the Castle Gardens (seen through the bridge, with St Mary's Church beyond), taking in the view on their way home. *(Leics. Museums)*

With the river immediately to the west of the main line and the elevated approach from the north limiting options, the Railway was forced to site its goods warehouses, sidings and then engine shed, to the east of the line and south of the station but very separate from it. Laid out on the large finger of land between river and canal, the main goods warehouse is nearing completion in the late 1890s, with most lines in place and the first three horse drays having been delivered from Thompson McKay & Co. Ltd. A loading crane can be seen in position beyond the drays. *(Leics. Museums)*

for attention, being seen on the GCR before being noted on the Midland. Even to the end, when taken over by the Midland Region of BR, one was never quite sure what would be on shed and the sight of such as the Gas Turbine prototype GT3, standing under the sheerlegs at the side of the shed building in 1961, was ever a bonus.

The Great Central of a whole was a mixed set of circumstances, the original lines, North of Sheffield, being marked by hundreds of daily coal trips trundling prodigious loads of coal principally from the Barnsley area to the Sheffield and Manchester areas. South of Nottingham it was a more streamlined system which allowed the not inconsiderable traffic between Nottinghamshire and London a clear run on a mainline which was almost wholly bereft of goods lines. Indeed once a southbound coal train left Nottingham Victoria there was little one could do with it other than to keep it going. On the neighbouring Midland matters were quite different, much of the route being enhanced with goods lines where slow moving traffic could be kept clear of

passenger services. It was this difference between the two that contributed to the Great Central's rather jaundiced reputation. A look at the passenger timetable suggested a very second class line with long gaps between trains. In truth one of the reasons the GC ran so little in the way of passenger traffic was because there was very little space for passenger services, which, it should be remembered, contributed less than one third of the income of a busy system.

A consideration of the route's goods services gives a different picture entirely and the frequency of trains between the Nottingham area and Woodford, where most trains were remarshalled and re-engined before entering the London district, was dense and called for especial operating disciplines. One such was the introduction of the Windcutters: coal trains which ran to accelerated timings between Annesley and Woodford in order to reduce line occupation. A critical feature of the scheme was the punctual start of servcies from Annesley and any engine ringing out late from the shed was sent back, the train cancelled with the culprit in danger of the disciplinary procedure. Drivers were paid a bonus for running the trains and this, together with the derived interest in the plan, contrived to reduce the incidence of late starts to a level that many other yards would have envied. Once on the road the trains were watched with keen interest from the GC control room at Nottingham and every attempt made to keep a clear road for them.

Leicester, curiously enough for a major manufacturing city, was not given any

marshalling facilities by the GC and what goods activity there was, was centred on the GC goods depot which ran occasional daily trips to the outlying stations and sidings to bring traffic in for inclusion on the handful of services which orinigated in the City. Almost all other GC freight services ran through the area, stopping only at Loughborough for water before terminating at Woodford. The principal express goods workings were those in connection with the East coast fish traffic, running from Hull and Grimsby to Banbury together with a nightly service in each direction between Manchester and Marylebone. One interesting service was an up night train which ran through from Glasgow to Marylebone, leaving the NER at York. There was no corresponding northbound working.

Apart from the freight traffic, which remained healthy and substantial to the end, the passenger trains were never heavily laden, largely due to the rural nature of the route, but also to the competition at those stations which did serve larger conurbations - Lutterworth was the only town on the route not to have been served already by another railway. Aylesbury was well served by the Metropolitan Railway; Rugby by the LNWR; and Leicester, Loughborough, Nottingham and Sheffield by the Midland; and the Marylebone-Manchester expresses, although fast, did have the disadvantage of having to travel by way of Sheffield and the Woodhead route, not exactly direct and not giving much competition to the more straightforward LNW line via Crewe from Euston. At its height, there were fourteen trains reaching Leicester from London, nine of them being expresses and giving a fastest time of 108 minutes, a mere three minutes longer than the Midland rival over a route four miles longer, but the Central still had this problem with lack of populated centres. Northwards from Leicester, the Midland slipped to second place, the route to Nottingham being four miles longer and the fastest train being on average five minutes longer than the Central non-stoppers; but the damage was done with the rest of the route and there never really was any competition. The post-Grouping absorption by the LNER and 'relegation' to second-class main line status within that organisation as it sought to recover from the ravages of the War and the post-hostilities' deprivations, brought a less caring approach to motive power needs on the GCR, with a resultant perceived and actual diminution in its importance. This was despite a sop to the ex-GC operation by way of naming two of the line's expresses. The 'Master Cutler', from Sheffield to Marylebone, was introduced on 6 October 1947, followed some seven months later, on 31 May 1948, by the 'South Yorkshireman', stretching the connections even further, by starting its run at Bradford. However, that further rationalisation and reorganisation be wrought by the 1948 Nationalisation on the GCR was, perhaps, inevitable, bearing in mind that the 'London Extension' line was in truth little more than a duplication of existing routes and, apart from some very useful work by-passing heavily bombed conurbations during the Second World War, there was nothing really vital to ensure its continued existence. In 1950, the empire was partially disintegrated, the infrastucture being taken over by the LMR whilst operations and motive power remained in ER hands until 1960 when the London Midland assumed full responsibility for the whole route.

The 'Master Cutler' was transferred to the King's Cross route from Sheffield followed by the cessation of the through day Marylebone-Manchester expresses in 1961. Local services also ceased at about this time leaving only a handful of semi-fast trains in operation between London and Nottingham. The Gresley pacifics which had been responsible for the express services under ER administration returned to their native metals and were replaced by Stanier 5MT 4-6-0s and, in particular, BR standard 5MT locomotives. From 1961, once the class 40 diesels had gained a foothold on the West coast mainline, the GC saw a return of large engines, this time being redundant 7P 4-6-0s and Britannia pacifics. Little of their former powers remained and the performances put up on the Nottingham trains was, to say the least, dismal by these engines which were generally in poor condition. Eventually the Black 5s returned for the final couple of years and

Above. **The warehouse in the last view can be seen again, right, beyond the signal gantry, across the main line tracks, in this view from around 1898. Squeezed onto a narrow spit of land between the River Soar, extreme left of picture, and the main line, is a carriage shed under construction. Looking like two air-raid shelters side-by-side, there would eventually be four tracks, accommodating some of the many coaches that would be required by the railway and Leicester in particular, for both local and longer distance services. To the left is the block of stables, to be home to the fleet of horses that were utilised in the early days, often for local deliveries. The gentleman, centre, is obviously in some supervisory capacity and is keeping an eye on the two navvies in the wagon, left. Note the wagons on the shed road are on loan from the Midland Railway, but the significance of the white cross on one buffer is unknown. When Vic Berry was developing his scrap metal business on this site in the late-1980s/early-1990s, he had plans to turn the carriage shed into a paint shop. During his excavation, preparatory to laying floor screed, he uncovered the four pits installed by the GCR for inspecting the rakes of coaches within the shed confines, all still in excellent condition. (Leicesters Museums)**

Below. **Time has moved on and the railway is virtually ready for routine operation. An obviously brand-new and spacious signal box, the paintwork of green and cream (?) still fresh, has been situated hard by the carriage shed (seen to the right) and is designated, rather grandly, 'Leicester Goods Yard North Cabin'. Responsibilities would include overseeing the signal gantry seen in the last view, controlling the northern approach to the Goods Yard sidings, as well as the turnouts themselves, two seen in the foreground of this shot, and acceptance of trains heading north for the station. Note the discarded pointwork in the foreground, the coal supplies for the signalman's stove (and carriage shed heating?), and the factory, left, standing on Western**

remained in harness until the end of mainline running in 1966.

After this a pathetically poor substitute of a diesel multiple-unit was introduced onto the Rugby-Nottingham stretch of line, the rest of the route north and south being closed, but this, calling at unmanned and rapidly deteriorating stations did little to encourage traffic and the plug was finally pulled on 3 May 1969, when a large crowd gathered on the desolate Leicester central platforms to see the last train depart and to mourn the dismal and sad end to a once glorious vision. As for freight, this once-proud tradition saw a slower and less protracted death. Traffic in the main commodities mentioned above saw something of a downturn, especially in the steel carrying loads and with the improvement of the Midland route via Birmingham in the early 1960s, the 'trunk' NE/SW axis through Banbury had less relevance, leading to an announcement from the British Railways Board on 26 February of intention 'of' closure of the GCR to freight officially on 5 April 1965, although freight trains did continue to run after this date. The last booked freight south of Leicester was an Abbey Lane sidings to Fawley empty petrol tanks train, on 11 June 1965, hauled by Standard 2-10-0 92032. Leicester South Goods signal box

Access to the goods yard from the south was by way of sidings branching off the main line close by the engine shed and then running northwards, passing under Upperton Road bridge. This bridge and the sidings, with a healthy consist of traffic, can be seen beyond another WR visitor on Monday, 15 August 1960. 4993 *Dalton Hall*, a rare interloper from Worcester (85A) shed, gathers speed with its easy-loaded six-coach 5.20 p.m. stopper to Woodford Halse. *(Horace Gamble)*

closed the following day. What goods traffic there was to the Central area at Western Boulevard, in Leicester, was then coped with by way of a spur from the Midland's Burton-on-Trent line, put in the early summer of 1965 for that purpose

and tripped from the Midland shed. Understandably, and not surprisingly, local M.P.s and a great many Leicester people protested at the plans and what they saw as 'a murder' of the line, but their pleas and exhortations came to

This is the view, looking north from Upperton Road bridge in 1964, and is a wonderful depiction of the extent of the ex-GC goods yard, with the warehouse boldly squat, centre, and carriage sheds, stables and the Goods Yard North Cabin across the tracks, all still in existence, although not all in active use. Freight has but a year to survive on the main line, but goods yard trade appears healthy enough, with coal, stone and much else besides in the wharves, right, leading up to Western Boulevard. Indeed, such was the current demand after the Central closed to freight in 1965, that a spur was put in from the ex-Midland route to Coalville, that crossed over the GC south of Upperton Road by the old engine shed. To serve brothers Vic and Frank Berry, amongst others, in their respective scrap businesses, the spur was still in occasional use into the 1990s. Vans and lorries stand on Western Boulevard, to the right of the old warehouse, ready to trip produce into the city. *(David Webb)*

Fifty years of use have seen some 'weathering ' of brickwork and glass of Leicester Central Shed - not surprising in view of the presence of spuming railway engines and the exigiencies of the Power Station across the river, in the background! Date unknown, but obviously in the very early days of Nationalisation, two appie green liveried B1s, 1109 and 61311, simmer quietly between duties in the bright mid-afternoon sunshine. Note that the 3 ft. diameter clock, initially situated centrally in the stone capping to the shed front, has perforce been moved to a position above the office front door, a victim of grime and inaccessibility.

nothing. A few preservationists, under the banner of 'The Main Line Steam Trust', had come together in 1968, an eye on preserving the line and restoring some sort of service, but their plans came to nought within the city boundaries and, apart from the street level frontage - minus clock tower - and the remnants of a former office block with Flemish-style gable ends, at platform level, that still remain, the Central station buildings were demolished in 1971, giving to way to industrial units, approached by way of a ramp road from the street level, smashed through part of the old retaining wall and up over the site of the station turntable! There have been rumours of thoughts/plans to re-open the line through the city as a Light Rail option - indeed, in 1989, the County Council decided space should be reserved in a proposed development in Bede Island, to allow for a line out to Glen Parva and surrounding areas, utilising the GC trackbed - but it is hard to see the economics of this, despite the strangulation of traffic on the streets below by cars/lorries, etc., especially considering the need to rebuild much of the viaduct both north and south of the station complex and it is likely, therefore, that this option will unfortunately continue to be a mere pipe-dream. Thus, a once-proud Railway, born

out of enthusiasm and vision, but already an anachronism by the time it was completed, was to be emasculated and raped at the bitter whim of petty politics, with its potential probably never being fully realised. In the early years of the 1990s, there has been much speculation over the possibility of a business consortium re-opening the length from Verney Junction to Lutterworth, in connection with a Channel Tunnel freight village near the northern end. With the easy gradients and generous loading gauge, this would seem an ideal prospect and one which whets the appetite for fast-running again over the route, albeit with modern traction and not the glorious steam locomotives that plied their trade along the line for so long.

As the second half of the final decade of this century dawns, there is still, however, a small remnant of ex-GC land within the city boundaries is still in use. In 1965, a spur was built adjacent to the old shed site, linking the Midland route to Burton-on-Trent to the GC, to enable trains to access the scrap metal sites on Western Boulevard, occupying the previous Central goods yard. The area achieved fame in the mid- to late-1980s, as Vic Berry operated there for a decade, refurbishing stock as well as scrapping and being one of the very few sites given

sanction for stripping asbestos. He piled stock high for a period, as this was being flushed from BR at a rapid rate and his site became another tourist attraction! Sadly, this all came to an end in a massive fire in the early hours of March 10, 1991 and what now remains is a much smaller operation run by another scrap merchant, but trains still visit the site, maintaining a slim link to the past.

Right. **One of the delights of the GC and one of its problems, was that it passed through much scenic terrain, but precious little in the way of large conurbations, certainly south of Sheffield. Consequently, the race-track was ideal for fast freights, but passenger services were hard pushed, even in the halcyon pre-motor car days, to break even, let alone attract large numbers of travellers. The sylvan view, therefore, of railway crossing canal was symptomatic of the Railway's pleasure and pain. On a dull Wednesday, 13 July 1966, 'Black 5' 44835 crosses the Leics. & Northants Union Canal near Aylestone, accelerating away from Leicester with the 8.20 a.m. Nottingham Victoria - Rugby Central semi-fast service. The chalked message on the smokebox door is unclear, but could it refer to the ending of this steam-hauled service in less than two months?** *(Horace Gamble)*

Leicester Central shed under construction in red brick by Henry Lovatt of Wolverhampton in the late 1890s, but already home to a locomotive, presumably one used by the contractors. The style of shed building is recognisably Great central and most of the depots built for the 'London Extension' were of very similar design; Leicester, provided with four roads, had potential accommodation for twenty engines. The foreman's office had a superb view of the yard and was spacious for its day; indeed, many of the depots still in use in the 1990s have smaller (and less opulent) accommodation! The overall facility occupying 10 acres, building is here still very much on the go, with the piles of materials, right, covering ground that will eventually become sidings. Its existence lasted 75 years, it being demolished in 1974, ten years after closure. *(Leicesters Museums)*

Tailpiece

The 13.12 Nottingham - St.Pancras train departs Leicester on August 16 1980. Photograph: Gavin Morrison.